100 IDEAS THAT CHANGED FASHION

Harriet Worsley

100 IDEAS THAT CHANGED FASHION

Harriet Worsley

Laurence King Publishing

Introduction

Life's formative moments often come when one least expects them. As an unworldly 12-year-old, I was offered the chance to explore my grandmother's wardrobe, and an entirely new and dazzling world opened up before me: silks and furs and velvet, and, so it seemed to me, numerous excuses for dressing up. There were boxy 1960s silk shift dresses in every imaginable colour, neat tweed suits and long velvet evening gowns. I was utterly captivated – and have remained so ever since. Vintage clothes have a history, and stories. There is something magical about holding a 1920s beaded silk flapper dress and imagining who wore it and what secrets it has within its folds: forgotten dances at wild parties? Secret love affairs?

My grandmother's clothes not only opened my eyes to the richness and variety of women's clothing, but, importantly, to the enormous distance that fashion itself had travelled. Like human evolution, women's fashions had adapted through countless stages to become the clothing that she wore. It was evident, looking at the well-crafted but simple luxury of those clothes from the 1950s and 1960s, so far removed from the fusty Victoriana of just 50 years before, that something dramatic happened to fashion in the first half of the twentieth century; and the remaining years proved no less exciting.

The twentieth century was one rich in innovation. It gave life to hundreds of new ideas and inventions, many of which had an impact on women's clothing. The sartorial contrast between the beginning and the end of the century is extreme. From the corsets, sweeping dresses and chaperoned women of 1900 to nude sunbathing, miniskirts, air travel and Internet shopping just 100 years later, it hardly seems possible that so much changed, and so fast.

The aim of *100 Ideas That Changed Fashion* is to highlight and explain these revolutionary changes in womenswear from 1900 to 2010. The ideas are presented chronologically, and are positioned in the book's fashion timeline to mark a point of change. For example, the T-shirt was worn in the early twentieth century as men's underwear, and was a mainstream fashion item during the second half of the century, so it appears in the book at the point that it became worn as outerwear – during the 1950s. The book sets out to encourage the reader to look at everyday clothes with a more informed eye: knowing that the first bikini was deemed so outrageous that only a stripper would model it, that T-shirts were initially men's underwear and that the rivets on jeans were developed to strengthen workmen's trousers during the gold-rush era.

The book's objective, at its inception, rested on what would constitute an 'idea', about which there was much debate. We concluded that each idea had to be something that rerouted the course of fashion and without which womenswear would not be what it is today.

The most obvious ideas were the new inventions. These ranged from relatively small fashion-specific entities such as the zip or nylon to more far-reaching inventions such as the computer and air travel. Such inventions could not be ignored, but the book's focus is squarely on how fashion changed as a result of these brilliant leaps forward, rather than on the inventions themselves.

Fashion's reaction to major political or economic world events also had to be included, for the effect they had on the course of fashion was irrefutable. The Great Depression of the 1930s led women to copy costume trends from Hollywood movies as a means of escapism from those dark days, while the restriction of materials during World War II led to the evolution of new fashion ideas such as streamlined suits and wooden- and cork-soled shoes.

The emancipation of women was one of the greatest changes of the twentieth century, and its effect on fashion was immense and far-reaching. As society allowed women to do more for themselves – to go out to work, to vote, and, in the case of society women, to ditch their chaperones – clothing had to adapt. An independent unaccompanied woman clearly needed a handbag to carry her valuables.

More importantly, war work could hardly be done efficiently in a rib-compressing whalebone corset. Later, in the 1920s, competing against men in the workplace did not call for frilled dresses but, rather, for a plain skirt suit. The bias cut, the influence of sportswear and the introduction of synthetics all allowed women to dress with more comfort and ease, and to enjoy clothes suited to their increasingly dynamic lifestyles. Interestingly, many of these key innovations appropriated elements from menswear; being traditionally more casual, comfortable and practical, it was an obvious shift. Chanel was a great pioneer in this respect, adapting men's yachting trousers, jumpers and pea coats for women, while Yves Saint Laurent gave women the trouser suit, making it a respectable option for formal occasions.

Just as emancipated woman changed the course of fashion, so the arrival of the 'teenager' in the 1950s – a new, dynamic social force with spending power – created a different target market for designers and spawned numerous trends that feature as ideas in this book. Aside from mainstream teenage fashion, many youth-driven subcultural groups, with their own sartorial codes, blossomed from the middle of the century, ranging from 1960s mods and hippies to the skaters and indie kids of the 1990s. These in turn began to feed the creativity of designers, starting with Yves Saint Laurent in the 1960s, to Tom Ford, Anna Sui and many more in the 2000s, who were all creating luxury collections, and looking for new inspiration and energy.

The twentieth century saw a breaking down of the notion that dress codes demarcate social status, and this also threw up some interesting ideas for the book. Coco Chanel introduced the wealthy to the black dress and the suntan (which had formerly only been seen on working-class women), and persuaded society women that costume jewellery could be as acceptable as wearing real jewels. Meanwhile, the advent of mass-manufacturing, and an increase in social mobility, means that today the same trends can be enjoyed and worn by all, as the high-street stores knock out smart, affordable copies of the catwalk looks.

Fashion went truly global during the twentieth century, and this introduced a number of ideas to the book such as fashion's increasing use of motifs and silhouettes influenced by cultures outside the West; the emergence of Japanese designers on Western catwalks and the eclipse of Paris as the only credible centre of fashion. Today, fashion media, design, manufacturing and business operate internationally rather than nationally. The Internet spreads the fashion gospel worldwide, with the live streaming of fashion shows, as well as blogs, magazines and shopping sites.

Fashion designers themselves are included in this book only in relation to their best innovations. The very greatest designers and business giants, the arbiters of change, all merit a mention for their contribution to fashion – Coco Chanel, Elsa Schiaparelli, Yves Saint Laurent, Vivienne Westwood, Calvin Klein, John Galliano, Tom Ford and more.

While working on this book I gave birth to my daughter, Jessie. At the time, newspaper reports were claiming that this new generation, hers, could easily live for 100 years. What changes will she see in her lifetime? If the developments in the last 110 years have been extreme, then imagine the year 2110. The final idea in this book hints at the futuristic surprises that are just beginning now – computers integrated into clothing, and prints that change on a skirt with the push of a button. But what's coming next? If the last century is anything to go by, it is certainly destined to be challenging, dramatic and unlike anything we can possibly imagine today.

Made to measure for the super-rich

COUTURE

Couture clothes are made to measure for a specific woman's body size, as opposed to ready-to-wear clothes that are made in standard sizes. We would not have haute couture without Charles Frederick Worth, its founding father.

Lady Curzon in the Peacock Dress of 1909 by Charles Frederick Worth, the first couturier. He designed show-stopping gowns for royalty, actresses and the nouveaux riches.

Until the 1960s, the Paris couturiers led European fashion trends, largely defining the way in which women dressed. While the relevance of haute couture today is debatable, owing to its vast expense and limited client-base, before the 1960s couture designers played an essential role as trend-makers and -breakers.

Worth was the first designer to make his name as a fashion star. Born in Lincolnshire, England, in 1825, he moved to Paris at the age of 20, where he set up his own fashion house in 1858. It was the first designer atelier. The fashionable Empress Eugénie, wife of Napoleon III, took him under her wing, and thereafter Worth quickly became the darling of society. He made his name designing ostentatious gowns for royalty and the nobility, actresses and the nouveaux riches, and his business flourished. Worth had no time for shawls, bonnets and other such frippery – he focused on flattering the female figure, swathing it in luxurious fabric. He was especially fêted for his white tulle evening dresses.

The haute couture industry of today is Worth's abiding legacy. He was a great innovator, becoming the first to show clothes on live models, and the first to present a new collection every year. His garments were customized to each client and patiently adapted to her whims. In the manner of an artist, Worth even signed his dresses by hand.

Worth's successors, the couturiers of the early twentieth century, united in 1910 to form the Chambre Syndicale de la Couture Parisienne. This group actively promoted its clothes to overseas markets, and paved the way for the biannual couture shows that are staged in Paris today.

Until the 1990s the Chambre Syndicale had very strict rules of admission, but these rules have been relaxed recently to allow younger designers in. With members including John Galliano for Christian Dior, and such mavericks as Jean Paul Gaultier and Viktor & Rolf, couture today is anything but dull. It is a quirky mix of fantastical and wearable pieces, and showcases the meticulous work of some of fashion's most expert crafts-people. The relevance of haute couture in the modern world may still be a subject of heated debate, but its drama and creativity are undeniable. ∎

A John Galliano design for Christian Dior couture, Spring/Summer 2007.

The lure of the fame game

BELOW: *Model, celebrity and fashion icon Kate Moss in New York City, 2009. Her modelling career, influential sense of style and her clothing ranges for Topshop have made her a household name.*

BOTTOM: *Audrey Hepburn wears a costume by Hubert de Givenchy on the set of* Sabrina, *1953.*

IDEA Nº 2
CELEBRITIES

We unquestionably live in a celebrity-obsessed society. Television cameras and paparazzi lenses ensure that the lives of the rich and famous are thrust upon us in almost every medium, whether it be television, online news, magazines or social media.

And we can watch celebrities' fashion triumphs and disasters as they happen, **the Internet** enabling information to be streamed to our homes at lightning speed. Throughout history, prominent people have always exerted tremendous sway in fashion. Royalty, actresses and royal mistresses have all been trend-setters. The first couturier, Charles Frederick Worth, benefited from the high-profile patronage of fashion icon Empress Eugénie, the wife of Napoleon III of France. During the 1900s society beauties and actresses were pictured on postcards and cigarette cards in order to show off new fashions. From the beginning of the twentieth century, celebrities started to play a crucially important role in fashion – by patron-izing designers and, in wearing their clothes, giving prominence to their designs. Rather than on television or the Internet, reports appeared in news-papers and magazines.

By the 1930s women were flocking to the movies and copying the influ-ential looks of Hollywood stars – Greta Garbo's trench coats, Joan Crawford's full painted lips, Marlene Dietrich's smouldering glamour. And the film studios' costume designers, such as Travis Banton and Gilbert Adrian, ensured that the stars looked as impec-cable off-screen as they did on it.

Prominent actresses and fashion designers have often formed highly successful mutually beneficial relation-ships, with the success of each raising the other's profile. A perfect example was the long-standing pairing of actress Audrey Hepburn and designer Hubert de Givenchy, notably for her clothes for the 1954 movie *Sabrina*, but just as importantly for the neat black trousers and bateau-necked tops that Hepburn wore off-screen.

Giorgio Armani's designs for Richard Gere in *American Gigolo* (1980) raised his profile, and popularized the loose, wide-shouldered jacket. Today Keira Knightley has teamed up with Chanel, and Scarlett Johansson with Louis Vuitton, with the stars featuring in the brands' advertising campaigns and wearing their clothes off-screen.

More than ever, designers are clamouring to dress movie stars for red-carpet events such as the Oscars. And with an increasingly media-hungry public, and the currency of celebrity being somewhat cheapened, the fashion houses are busier than ever trying to seduce the major stars of the moment with their designs. ∎

1930s film star Marlene Dietrich poses with a cigarette. Her tailored suits and languid beauty were legendary.

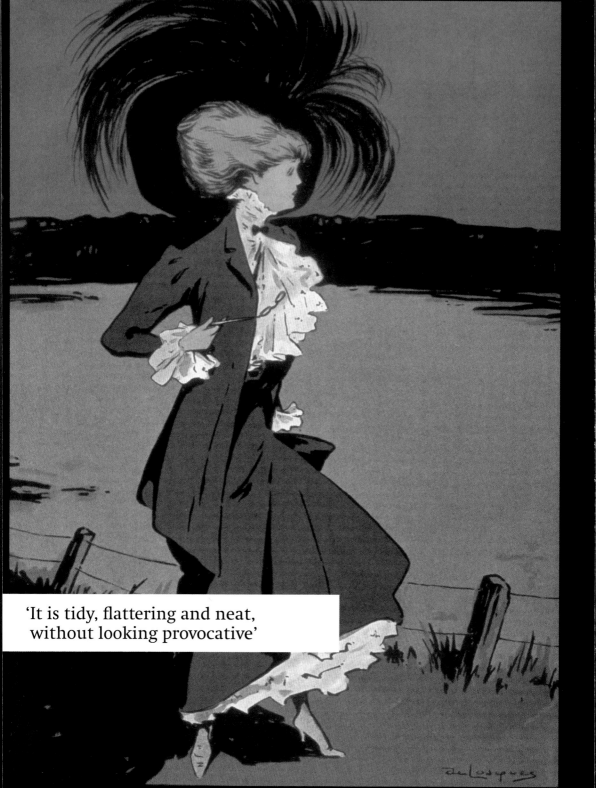

'It is tidy, flattering and neat,
 without looking provocative'

The essential uniform for the working woman

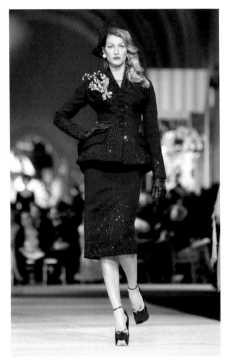

IDEA № 3

THE SKIRT SUIT

Fashionable women have been wearing suits since the seventeenth century – but only when on horseback. It was not until the end of the nineteenth century that suits were adopted for wear outside the equestrian world.

Skirt suits, or tailor-mades as they were known, comprising a jacket or coat worn over a blouse and a long sweeping skirt, were worn by ladies in the early twentieth century for social calls and shopping expeditions.

Queen Alexandra, wife of King Edward VII of Britain and a fashion icon of her generation, became renowned for her sleek travel suits by her favourite tailor, John Redfern. The style was modern for the time, and feminists wore them to make a political point, in rejecting the femininity of sweeping dresses. This was, of course, an early precursor to the trouser suit of the 1960s. By the outbreak of World War I, working women had started to wear the coat and skirt. It was durable and practical, and pretty dresses suddenly seemed inappropriate for the office.

By the end of the 1930s, women of all classes had taken up the tailored streamlined skirt suit. They married in them and worked in them. In 1942 prominent British designers, including Norman Hartnell and Hardy Amies, designed sharp-shouldered women's suits as part of the UK government's mass-produced Utility range, which conformed to the stringent fabric and design constraints of the war, such as restricted pleats and shorter skirts.

After the boxy skirt suits of the 1960s, which hung away from the body, the suit really came into its own again during the 1980s. Thierry Mugler and Claude Montana perfected the working woman's power suit, with its tight skirt and jacket with wide masculine shoulders. Donna Karan devised her own softer working woman's capsule wardrobe, with her all-in-one leotard-style 'body', and flattering interchangeable wrap-around skirts and blazers. Today the skirt suit is the standard working uniform for professional women. It is tidy, flattering and neat, without looking provocative. ∎

Liberation for women

IDEA № 4

THE DEATH OF THE CORSET

In the early years of the twentieth century, respectable women in Europe and the United States took great pride in squeezing their bodies into unnaturally curvaceous shapes. They had to suffer in order to look beautiful.

American actress Camille Clifford shows off her corset-bound figure in the early 1900s. Over a century later reality TV star Kim Kardashian's exaggerated hour-glass curves became part of her brand image.

Their torsos were squashed into corsets, which were stiffened with metal or whalebone and tightened brutally hard with laces. With pads added to the hips and under the arms to exaggerate a tiny waistline, a full-length skirt finished off the look.

In the United States, the ideally proportioned woman of the era was popularized by the illustrator Charles Dana Gibson, and his drawings were personified most famously by the curvy actress Camille Clifford. Today, her wasp-waisted figure looks almost grotesquely distorted. Yet not all women were prepared to suffer the discomfort of a corset. The suffragettes of England began a campaign against these restrictive garments in 1904, and soon afterwards the French followed suit.

Salvation was at hand. In 1906 the French fashion designer Paul Poiret introduced a ground-breaking softer silhouette, inspired by the eighteenth-century empire-line style, which rendered extreme corsetry redundant. A Poiret skirt fell straight to the floor from a high empire-line band, which sat just under the bust. With no need of a tiny waist any more, women could breathe freely again. Poiret himself was keenly aware of the social implications of his innovation: 'It was equally in the name of Liberty that I proclaimed the

downfall of the corset and the adoption of the brassiere,' he wrote. Poiret's fluid gowns were startlingly different from the rustling silks and bustles of the Victorian era. Other designers, including Madeleine Vionnet and the House of Paquin, also promoted the new look.

Nonetheless, women did not do away with control underwear completely. While whalebone stays were no longer desirable, tube corsets were still favoured: woven elastic, which pulled in the hips, flattened the stomach and liberated the bust. These were far from perfect, as they restricted movement in the legs. With the advent of World War I, women started to work in jobs that had traditionally been the preserve of men, and stretch corsets became correspondingly shorter in order to allow more mobility. Eventually, the modern choice became the stretch girdle, which just held in the hips, worn with a bra. ∎

This 1911 engraving from Les Robes de Paul Poiret *by Georges Lepape depicts Poiret's new languid, empire-line silhouette.*

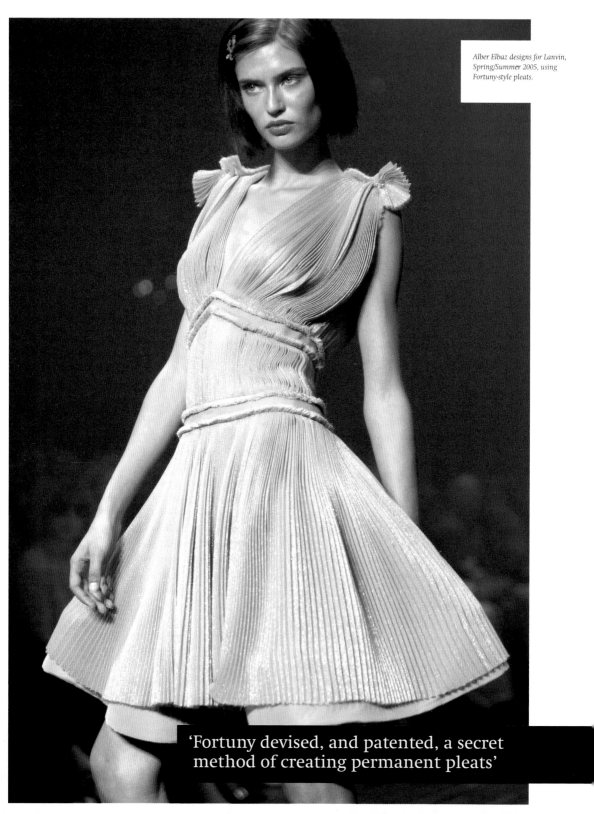

'Fortuny devised, and patented, a secret method of creating permanent pleats'

IDEA № 5

THE DELPHOS GOWN

The Spanish designer Mariano Fortuny revolutionized fashion with his legendary Delphos gown of 1907 by offering women an alternative to structured dressing. Although he worked as a fashion designer, he regarded himself primarily as a painter, artist and inventor.

Actress and singer Régine Flory wears a Delphos gown by Mariano Fortuny in 1910.

His aim was to celebrate the female form through dress. He clothed both the unorthodox Russian ballet dancer Anna Pavlova and the modern dancer Isadora Duncan, who caused scandal with her unconventional views and her semi-nudity on-stage.

The pleated silk-satin Delphos gown could be rolled or twisted to fit into a tiny box. Once removed, it would stretch out again into a full-length dress, with its pleats intact. Fortuny devised, and patented, a secret method of creating permanent pleats, which involved laying wet, folded silk on heated porcelain tubes. His dresses hung from the shoulders while moulding to the body, without using conventional seams. The bright dye used to colour the dresses was sometimes graded, so that the colours seemed to melt into each other, and a tied silk cord drew in the fabric at the waist or neckline. Delicate Murano glass beads from Venice acted both as decorative devices and to weight veils and hems.

Fortuny's Delphos gown stemmed from his passionate interest in Greek antiquity and the English Aesthetic Movement. He named the dress after his inspiration, a famous ancient Greek sculpture, the life-sized bronze *Charioteer of Delphi*.

The Delphos gown appealed to newly liberated women, who wanted to express themselves and move freely, without the restrictions of corsets or stiff dresses. The dresses were modern, flattering, and elongated the figure. They were initially worn only for entertaining at home, and women didn't dare to wear them in public until the 1920s. The Parisian designer Madeleine Vionnet also shared a passion for ancient Greece, and introduced bias-cut draped dresses for high-society ladies. Later, American designer Mary McFadden experimented with pleated fabrics in the style of Fortuny, and later still, the **Japanese design**er Issey Miyake took up the Fortuny mantle with his Pleats Please collections, first launched in 1993. The Fortuny legacy lives on. ∎

Push-up and plunge

IDEA Nº 6
THE BRA

While rudimentary bras, known as bust supporters, started to be worn as early as the 1880s, it was not until 30 years later that they began to make true fashion sense. This was due to the new empire-line silhouette of the 1910s.

This ground-breaking style looked best when worn over a girdle or a shortened corset that stopped above the waist, together with a separate brassière. Between 1890 and 1917 Samuel Gossard, Rose Kleinert, Gabrielle Poix and a handful more secured successful patents for their own versions of the brassiere. The best-known patent was by American Mary Phelps Jacob (later known by her more seductive married name, Caresse Crosby) who put forward a simple design in 1914 – two hand-kerchiefs held together by strips of ribbon. Her brassiere looked pretty, but was by no means supportive for the well-endowed.

By the 1920s most women had adopted the brassiere in bandeau form – a flattening, bandage-style bra that squashed down the breasts to help create the desired boyish silhouette of the era. New companies such as Lovable and Maiden Form catered for the demand for bras. The new cup sizes, padding and boning of the 1930s gave increased support; **nylon**, the durable and lightweight wonder-fibre, proved ideal for 1940s designs.

The curvaceous starlets of 1950s America such as Jayne Mansfield took full advantage of increasing support in bra design. The latest versions pushed the breasts up and out to a near point. These busty beauties inspired a generation of teenage girls to adopt the 'sweater girl' look – a tight jumper worn over an arrestingly protruding bust. While some 1960s women really did go braless, Rudi Gernreich offered them an alternative with his No-Bra

Bra of 1964, which gave transparent coverage but little breast support. Other designers followed in the 1970s with light bras made from sheer fabric.

By the 1990s full support was back, and the Wonderbra, which pushed the breasts up into firm globes, became a best-seller, aided by the notorious advertising campaign that featured model Eva Herzigová and the strapline 'Hello Boys'. The lingerie company Agent Provocateur, co-founded by Vivienne Westwood's son Joseph Corré in 1994, helped to put sex back into smalls in the UK, with luxury collections of underwear sold from shops with strikingly raunchy window displays, more often associated with the red light district than with respectable shopping areas of the time. The bust supporter had come a long way. ∎

TOP: *An early bra, Paris 1930s.*

ABOVE: *American movie star Jayne Mansfield flashes her well-supported breasts during a night out in Hollywood in 1951.*

Bra and matching underwear set by luxury lingerie company Agent Provocateur, 2010.

Sharon Tate marries Roman Polanski in 1968 in a white minidress. After the 1920s a wedding dress was expected to be white, but the cut could be dictated by fashion.

The only colour for a bride

THE WHITE WEDDING DRESS

Queen Victoria's controversial white wedding dress caught the imagination of romantic 19th-century brides and was to influence wedding dress fashion throughout the 20th century.

When the young Queen Victoria married her cousin Albert in 1840, she was hailed as a true romantic. Unusually for royalty, this was not a marriage of political convenience, but a genuine love match. The bride chose not to wear jewel-encrusted silver or gold robes as expected, but instead opted for a white satin and lace dress. And rather than a regal tiara, she simply wore orange blossom in her hair.

Traditionally, women had married in blue or pink or their favourite colour, making a wedding dress a garment that they could then wear again. Working-class women frequently opted for practical black. But the young Queen Victoria's example was truly modern and attention-grabbing, and swiftly caught the public imagination. Quite soon, all new brides wanted to wear white for their big day. Initially, this was only possible for the rich, for who else could afford the luxury of a white dress that could only be worn a handful of times before showing its age?

By the 1920s, however, white was established as the only colour for a respectable Western bride. As class divisions gradually melted, it became harder to read a woman's position in society by her clothes. And if a lady could marry in white, why shouldn't her maid?

Thus the colour white quickly became the universal choice for bride's dresses, bringing with it associations of bridal purity and virginity. The colour blue, which had traditionally signified purity, came to be considered risqué for a bride. However, marrying in white would not always mean a long white dress. Bianca Jagger chose a tailored white skirt suit in the 1970s, while actress Sharon Tate married in a very short white minidress in 1968. More extreme was the actress Pamela Anderson, who tied the knot in a white bikini and high heels in Saint-Tropez in 2006.

Where previously a wedding dress might have been worn again, the modern bride will spend a huge sum on a dress designed to be used just once. It will probably be the most expensive gown she ever wears. Impractical, extravagant and to be worn a single time: for the modern bride, nothing but white will do. ∎

Movie star, princess and fashion icon Grace Kelly on her wedding day.

Style icons from parliament and palaces

IDEA № 8

ROYALS AND POLITICIANS

Royalty, senior politicians and politicians' high-profile wives exert a huge fashion influence on the public, helping to raise the profile of fashion designers, as well as spawning copy-cat looks on the street.

Icons such as Jacqueline Kennedy and Diana, Princess of Wales, have always had to strike a difficult balance, having to look at the same time respectable, classy and fashionable, while being prepared for the media to scrutinize – and judge – everything they wear.

Queen Alexandra, wife of Prince Edward (later Edward VII), was a regal style icon of the late nineteenth and early twentieth century, with her striking poodle haircut, jewelled dog-collar chokers and high-necked blouses and dresses. More influential still was Wallis Simpson, the American divorcée for whom King Edward VIII renounced his throne in 1936. Rather than ostracize this interloper, society women copied her classy, elegant style, notably her Mainbocher wedding dress and its blue colour (known as Wallis Blue). And they paid close attention when she famously quipped that a woman could never be too rich or too thin. 'I'm nothing to look at, so the only thing I can do is dress better than anyone else,' was how she summed up her passion for clothes.

The fairytale life of Grace Kelly, who became first a Hollywood star and then royalty, upon marrying Prince Rainier of Monaco, provided inspiration to an entire generation of women. They slavishly imitated Princess Grace's coolly elegant style and could emulate her look with a Kelly bag, which

Hermès named after her. In 1949 the screen goddess Rita Hayworth married Prince Aly Khan wearing a striking blue dress by Jacques Fath, a fashion that many copied. And perhaps most famously of all, there was Diana, Princess of Wales, who lived constantly under the media spotlight. The public first copied her spectacular wedding dress, then adopted her hairstyle, and later subjected her ever-changing wardrobe to constant critical scrutiny.

Few female politicians make it on to the style pages, but the wives of politicians certainly do. First Lady Jacqueline Kennedy single-handedly brought pillbox hats back into fashion, and women copied her signature boxy trapeze-style suits, gilt-chained handbags and minimalist shift dresses. Her husband, John F. Kennedy, jokingly introduced himself to the British Parliament as her husband. More recently Michelle Obama, the only black First Lady to grace the White House, caused a stir with her vibrant and brightly coloured wardrobe, and her swanlike white chiffon inauguration dress by Jason Wu. The model, singer and ex-girlfriend of Mick Jagger, Carla Bruni, who married the French President Nicolas Sarkozy in 2008, also brought an injection of style to politics, raising the fashion bar with her demure Dior coats, neat ballet pumps and, of course, perfect good looks. ∎

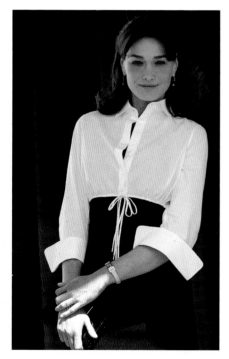

As wife to the French President, ex-model Carla Bruni-Sarkozy proves a stylish figure in public life.

LEFT: *First Lady Jacqueline Kennedy looks demure but effortlessly stylish in 1963.*

ABOVE: *The Duke and Duchess of Windsor in 1937. Wallis Simpson may have been blamed for the abdication of a king, but she was still revered as a style icon.*

'The magazines' pages served as disposable
galleries for fashion photographers' pictures'

*This striking photograph was taken
by Cecil Beaton for the October 1950
edition of UK Vogue.*

The first fashion shoots

ABOVE: *From a fashion shoot entitled 'The Birds' for* The Face, *February 1995.*

BELOW: *Writer and society beauty Nancy Mitford makes the cover of* The Bystander *in 1932.*

IDEA No 9

PHOTOGRAPHS IN MAGAZINES

Fashion magazines have always been illustrated – but until the latter part of the nineteenth century these illustrations were drawings. It took the introduction of photographs to bring the pages to life.

British photographic pioneer William Henry Fox Talbot introduced halftone printing in the 1850s and as the method was refined and commercialized over the next few decades, the impact on magazines was enormous. Fashionable ladies were now able to peruse the latest trends by means of excitingly realistic, full-colour, glossy photographs.

The *New York Daily Graphic* was the first newspaper to print a photograph, in 1873. The superiority of halftone printing over previous technology was obvious, and by the 1890s the process had spread to hundreds of publications. Halftone printing enables an image to be reproduced by breaking it down into a pattern of tiny dots, like a pointillist painting, using a series of fine mesh screens. The dots are of different sizes, which when seen from a distance are joined together by the human eye so that it appears to see a continuous-tone image – a photograph.

The ambitious launch of *Vogue* by American publishing company Condé Nast in 1909, and of the magazines that followed, such as *Harper's Bazaar*, spawned a new breed: the fashion photographer. The magazines' pages served as disposable galleries for their photographs, and the editors of these magazines were their new patrons. Condé Nast appointed Baron Adolphe de Meyer as the first salaried staff photographer in 1914. His job was to photograph not models but society ladies, whose fashionable clothing was displayed for *Vogue* readers to admire and emulate. De Meyer's style was flattering, with a strong emphasis on soft focus. He moved to *Harper's Bazaar* in 1923.

Fashion photography flourished with the experimental work of the early in-house photographers at *Vogue* and *Harper's Bazaar*, most notably Edward Steichen, George Hoyningen-Huene, Horst P. Horst and Cecil Beaton. They experimented with new techniques and composition, and set the tone for twentieth-century fashion photography, making it an integral part of the fashion industry we know today. ■

THE HON. NANCY MITFORD
The eldest daughter of Lord and Lady Redesdale, who is at work on a new novel.

From Bunny Hug to breakdance

IDEA № 10
DANCE DRESS

Fashion designers love their clothes to be worn and promoted by youthful beauties; and youthful beauties like nothing more than to party and – almost always – to dance. As dance fads evolve with the cultural developments of each decade, so canny designers create clothes to reflect the new spirit and to complement the new moves.

A tango craze swept Europe and North America in the 1910s, and women stalked the dancefloor in dresses with slit hems and draped armholes, and shoes with ribbon ankle straps or Cleopatra sandals trimmed with a cameo. With the Roaring Twenties came an obsession for frenetic jazz beats. Dances such as the Bunny Hug and Kickaboo were best performed in short straight-up-and-down dropped-waist dresses in bold colours (the daring showed their knees) – the beads and fringes shook and sparkled with the dancer, while the obligatory diamanté 'slave' bracelets remained tightly secured, high up on the biceps.

The wide skirts and neat bodices of the 1950s complemented rock-and-roll moves, the skirts swirling as the girls were twirled, with the petticoats providing for modesty if they were swung up into the air. When the disco craze exploded in the 1970s, girls wanted to shimmer and shine like exotic fish under the flashing lights and spinning mirror balls. They chose stretch boob tubes, halter-neck jump-suits and skin-tight shiny trousers, all worn with strappy sandals in gold or silver.

Brightly coloured loose unisex clothing was the look for the acid house parties and **raves** of the 1980s and early 1990s, with comfortable T-shirts, wide **jeans** and Day-Glo accessories for 24-hour ecstasy-fuelled dance marathons. **Hip hop** culture and breakdancing introduced a street-smart combination of bright, branded tracksuits, **trainers** with large laces, and loose stretch **sport**swear, with breakdancers often wearing **nylon** tracksuits, trainers and hooded tops. The energetic, athletic nature of the dancing meant that sportswear was ideal. Tracksuits were good for sliding on floors, and a bandana worn under a baseball cap was perfectly suited for head spins. As dance moves progress from the formal to the athletic, so the clothing adapts to suit the dancers and their changing moves. ∎

TOP: *1920s flappers danced furiously in beaded and fringed dresses that shook and sparkled as they moved.*

ABOVE: *London breakdancers in 1983 wearing denim, sportswear and trainers.*

*Women dancing at the disco
club Studio 54 in New York,
November 1977.*

'Girls wanted to shimmer and shine
like exotic fish under the flashing lights
and spinning mirror balls'

IDEA № 11

MODERN TRAVEL

Changing modes of travel in the twentieth century brought with them new dress codes and fashions. From automobiles and motorcycles to ocean liners and aeroplanes, the seemingly continual invention of new ways to get about called constantly for new clothes and designs to suit.

Dunhill's Motorities advertisement, 1904. The invention of the car prompted radical developments in women's outerwear in order to protect their eyes, hairstyles and clothes.

From 1905, the rich started to buy motor cars to use for travel. Previously, cars had been purchased for their novelty value. Those who could afford an early open-topped car needed to dress appropriately, in order to protect the hair, eyes and clothes. Vast dustcoats, bonnets trimmed with veils, gauntlet gloves and goggles helped to keep at bay the dirt thrown up from the road. Dunhill made leather travel clothing for women from 1901 and Louis Vuitton crafted its own luxury leather luggage, designed to fit into the new motor cars. In 1959 the company developed a protective coating for its cotton canvas bags and trunks, to repel the grime of airports and the road.

The first woman to fly across the Atlantic was Amelia Earhart, in 1928. Female pilots were the epitome of glamour, and none more so than Earhart, resplendent in her leather jackets, silk scarves and slim-fitting trousers. She had a complete collection of flying clothes made for her by Elsa Schiaparelli. Earhart launched a fashion line endorsed with her name, and achieved some renown for her simple, stylish, hard-wearing clothes. In 2008 Jean Paul Gaultier at Hermès paid homage to her with his Earhart-styled catwalk models. In the 1930s Schiaparelli introduced a lightweight travel bag for women to take with them on flights, complete with an easy-to-pack capsule wardrobe. It included dresses, hats and a reversible coat for day and evening.

As commercial flying became common, the air hostess – as she was then called – also made her mark on fashion. Now viewed as overtly sexist, their prescribed uniforms often included miniskirts, catsuits and even **hot pants**.

Motorcycle and scooter owners created their own new subcultures and styles. The 1950s bikers, the disaffected youth who raced bikes and toured the States, wore leather jackets, blue **jeans** and dashing white scarves, as made famous by Marlon Brando's outlaw biker in *The Wild One* (1953). A decade on, rockers took up black leathers as their bike uniform. Their rivals, the **mods**, preferred green military-style parkas, to protect their slick Italian-style suits from dust kicked up by their scooters.

Space travel is not yet available to all, but this too may one day generate its own distinctive fashion style. ∎

1970s air hostesses working for Southwest Airlines wear hot pants as their uniform. The Texan airline's motto was 'sex sells seats' and in-flight drinks had names such as Passion Punch and Love Potion.

Saying it loud and saying it proud

PROTEST DRESS

Why shout when you can wear your message on your sleeve and make just as great an impact? As an alternative to throwing yourself under a racehorse or going on hunger strike as the early twentieth-century suffragettes did, you could simply march wearing the movement's protest colours of white for purity, green for hope and purple for dignity.

ABOVE: *African American activist Angela Davis in 1971. Her Afro signals her support for the struggle for racial equality.*

BELOW: *Suffragette songsheet, 1911, in the movement's colours of purple, green and white.*

Dressing for protest frequently influences mainstream fashion. The Afro hairstyle, used at first as a badge of black pride, was famously flaunted by activists Stokely Carmichael and Angela Davis, and made fashionable by singer James Brown. It caught on from 1968, the year that the Black Panthers made their mark as activists, taking as their uniform Afros, Cuban heels and black leathers. Similarly, when in the 1960s Germaine Greer stated that 'bras are a ludicrous invention', it became a feminist statement to go braless – a gesture that quickly lost its political value, however, as it became generally acceptable for women to go without a bra in the 1960s and 1970s. And while the hippie movement started as an anti-Vietnam War movement, others soon adopted their loose, layered clothes simply to look fashionable.

Katharine Hamnett boosted sartorial protest with her 1984 Choose Life collection of bold message T-shirts advocating world peace and environmental issues. That was also the year in which, famously, she met Prime Minister Margaret Thatcher while wearing a T-shirt printed with the words '58% Don't Want Pershing' – a reference to the public opposition to American Pershing missiles being based in the UK. The photographers immortalized her protest on camera, and it was featured in the press the following day. Hamnett set a trend for protest and slogan T-shirts, and in 2003

sent T-shirts on to the catwalk bearing the words 'Stop War, Blair Out', as a reaction to the war in Iraq.

Dressing for protest is not just the domain of single-issue campaigners. The **punk** movement rejected many of society's norms for anarchy and anti-authoritarianism. Their safety-pin accessories and outlandish clothing spoke eloquently of their rebellious nature. Conversely, sometimes it's what you do not wear that can make the greatest impact. The animal-rights group PETA made waves with its notorious advertising campaigns in the early 1990s featuring attractive undressed **celebrities** coupled with the slogan 'I'd rather go naked than wear fur'. And to reinforce the message, PETA protesters carrying banners with the same slogan stripped naked at Paris Fashion Week in 2007 and stormed the catwalk. Be it through overdressing or nudity, fashion became an acceptable vehicle for protest. Clothes could be used to shock, not merely to flatter the female form. ∎

Holly Madison poses nude for People for the Ethical Treatment of Animals (PETA) in 2007.

Photo: Christopher Ameruoso www.chrisaphoto.com

From Poiret to Pucci

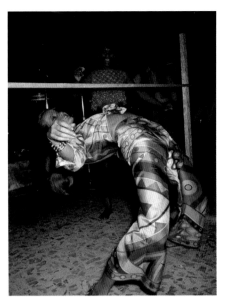

IDEA № 13

BOLD PRINTS

At the end of the nineteenth century, soft and delicate pastel shades were considered a sure sign of affluence, taste and gentility. But this demure approach to colour and design was not to last.

As the twentieth century wore on, women were no longer expected to look delicately self-effacing, and they gradually came to embrace bold colours and patterns as a form of self-expression. Paul Poiret gave fashion a jolt, introducing bright oriental colour, bold patterns and prints inspired by the Ballets Russes' appearance in Paris in 1909. Women wanted to embrace this new-found opulence and its youthful sense of fun.

Screen-printing was to revolutionize the textile-printing industry, as fashion fabrics could be printed using this technique. Although some prints were worn through World War II, it was during the 1950s that bright, breezy and optimistic prints took off, with stripes, florals and gingham printed on wide skirts and dresses. Even bolder were the bright swirling patterned silks of Italian aristocrat Emilio Pucci, who cornered the market for luxury casualwear and printed lightweight silk jersey dresses. He said: 'My prints are ornamental designs worked in continuous motion; however they are placed there is rhythm.'

Young people in the 1960s were drawn to bold prints, including Pop and Op art designs, the Mondrian-inspired work of Yves Saint Laurent, and loud florals and coloured stripes. Sonja Knapp went for a gentler approach with her soft prints in loud colours for the house of Ungaro. By the end of the decade, the hippie movement had inspired a move away from graphic patterns with patchwork, tie-dye, paisley prints, and influences from the Far East. Ossie Clark covered his light silk and satin dresses with organic flowing prints by his wife Celia Birtwell. British designer Zandra Rhodes made her name with voluminous silk dresses using Art Deco zigzag motifs.

Christian Lacroix opened his **couture** house in 1987, and shot to fame with his signature fabric embellished with bold prints, bright colour, beading and embroidery. Gianni Versace's baroque and Byzantine-inspired black and gold prints became highly desirable.

The graffiti print influenced a number of designers who wished to inject their work with an urban street feel, such as Viktor & Rolf, Moschino and Martin Margiela. Vivienne Westwood used prints by Keith Haring in 1983, while Stephen Sprouse collaborated with Marc Jacobs in the early 2000s and covered Louis Vuitton luggage and bags with his trademark graffiti motif. Once more, a luxury design house had borrowed from the street. ∎

ABOVE: *German countess and model Veruschka shows off her flamboyantly printed trousers and shirt by Emilio Pucci in 1966.*

BELOW: *1911 illustration for Les Ballets Russes by Léon Bakst. The dance company inspired fashion designers to use bold patterns and oriental references.*

The original style bible

IDEA № 14
VOGUE

By the end of the twentieth century, fashion magazines, their editors, and their staff had grown powerful, able to make or break a designer or a trend with a few careful words. The most powerful of all, *Vogue*, is renowned not only as the most influential fashion magazine but also as one of the most long-standing. It set a precedent in quality and style for the numerous fashion titles that have come after it, and is now published in 19 countries.

Arthur Baldwin Turnure founded *Vogue* as a small New York society weekly in 1892. But it was a young lawyer and publisher Condé Nast who turned the magazine around when he bought it on Turnure's death in 1909, adding more colour, advertisements and articles on society and fashion. He produced it fortnightly instead of weekly, started successful British and French editions (and also launched an unsuccessful version in Spain) and transformed *Vogue* into an exciting and glamorous fashion magazine aimed at affluent society women. Crucially, Nast also persuaded advertisers to pay big bucks to reach this discerning readership, making the magazine as lucrative as it was appealing.

In 1913 Nast hired the celebrated portrait photographer Baron Adolphe de Meyer as his staff fashion photographer, stepping up the glamour and style sections of the magazine. Photographs of society ladies in the latest frocks were always a staple feature of *Vogue*, but he now introduced fashion photographs of actresses and lively society beauties prepared to play to the camera.

When *Vogue* reached Britain in 1916, World War I was raging and public morale was low. Wartime was, however, good for magazine publishing. Women left behind while their menfolk were at the front could indulge in the escapism of *Vogue's* world of fashion and high society, and they were also keen to work on magazines as editorial staff. After the war ended, it was the new middle classes who lapped up fashion magazines.

Subscriptions boomed during the Great Depression and World War II. When the chips were down, it seemed, women bought *Vogue*. As the journalist Penelope Rowlands wrote in a biography of Carmel Snow, fashion editor of *Vogue* in the 1920s, 'Vogue was the summit, the apex, the *ne plus ultra* of the fashion world. It was, quite simply, It'. It was the biggest-selling American fashion magazine of all, she said: 'No other one could compete.' ■

UK Vogue *cover, July 1928.*

Paris Forecast & Clothes for Scotland

Broadening horizons

GLOBAL INFLUENCES

The dynamic nomadic style of designer John Galliano for his Autumn/Winter 2010 show.

Fashion designers working in the West use inspiration from other cultures and countries around the globe to enrich their collections. Whether gleaned from foreign travel, books or artefacts, the colours, prints, silhouettes or overall global themes help to inject new energy into fashion.

When the Ballets Russes first came dancing into Paris in 1909 they caused a sensation with their exotic and opulent costumes – not least the dancer Nijinsky, who was painted blue and wearing an eye-catching pair of Turkish trousers. The fashion designer Paul Poiret responded by injecting his work with exotic colour and oriental detailing, including turbans, plumes, kimonos and harem pants. They became the height of fashion, for those who dared to dabble in this extravagant world.

Thus inspired, designers went on to use Slavic folk prints in 1917 and, later, Egyptian and Chinese motifs. Between the wars, Chinese and Japanese details became fashionable. And after World War II, South American colours and prints influenced North American casualwear – they looked sunny and bold, perfect for the beach or the weekend.

With the arrival of affordable airline flights in the 1970s, world travel became easier and fashion influences from abroad flourished. **Hippies** came back from their Asian wanderings with embroidered waistcoats, Afghan coats, kaftans and gypsy tops. They roamed around in flowing skirts in bright colours and the loose, layered clothing worn in hot climates. Designers took note and, incorporating global styles from other cultures, they developed a luxury hippie aesthetic. One of Yves Saint Laurent's most memorable shows was the Russian collection of 1976, boasting exotic peasant boots, shawls and full swinging skirts. As Cecil Beaton observed of Saint Laurent in his diaries: 'His life in Marrakesh has

influenced him in cloth and thread embroidery. There are dull soft brocades with old thread in them that have all the restraint of early Persian art, and there are Chinese influences worked in garish colours ... It is unobtrusively elegant, different, new, uncompromising.'

Japanese designers including Issey Miyake and Yohji Yamamoto made an impact in the 1980s by employing wrapped and layered Eastern clothing. Versace concocted an Indian-inspired draped clothing collection while Rifat Ozbek included North American Indian feathers and beads – and prints inspired by Turkish Iznik tiles.

Romeo Gigli, Jean Paul Gaultier and John Galliano continue to absorb influences from around the globe. The latter's designs for Dior and his own label include fantastic concoctions, such as bright beaded collars inspired by the Masai people and dresses and vast kimono sleeves inspired by Japan. A collection from Galliano ensures a round-the-world tour, bringing beauty, rich ornament and spectacle to the catwalk. ∎

The decline of domestic service

D.I.Y. DRESSING

High society of the nineteenth and early twentieth century required complicated dress changes throughout the day: the day dress, the visiting dress, the tea gown, the evening dress. Waist-length hair had to be brushed out every night and artfully pinned up each morning, and corsets had to be laced up. None of this was possible without the help of a maid.

Upper- and middle-class households of the period took domestic service for granted, but World War I would change everything. In Britain, many working-class women left domestic service in order to fill what were traditionally male jobs. After the war, the middle classes tried to reclaim their servants, but without success. Former staff now wanted to remain in their civil-service, transport, factory or clerking jobs. They had enjoyed a taste of independence and the higher wages offered, and wished to better themselves in society.

In the 1920s, relaxed **sporty** clothes in dark colours (previously associated with the working classes) started to be worn by everyone. This meant less ironing, mending and washing; and dressing could be achieved at speed. Simple chignons or practical bobbed hair meant no more hours of fussing at the dressing table – shorter bobs, the Eton crop and the shingle were the fashionable styles, and boyishly simple to maintain.

While working-class women had a new taste of freedom in the workplace, middle- and upper-class women were freed from the fetters of elaborate, uncomfortable, time-consuming dress. 'The problems of quick dressing and the beginning of the lack of servants now became acute. Schiap made aprons and kitchen clothes so that American women could do their own cooking and still look attractive,' wrote Elsa Schiaparelli in her 1954 autobiography, *Shocking Life*.

Coco Chanel and Jean Patou inspired a modern and streamlined boyish silhouette for the Roaring Twenties. It was a world away from the bustles, corsets and sweeping dresses worn just 20 years before.

After World War II, the advent of refrigerators, vacuum cleaners and other labour-saving appliances meant less need for servants; and, moreover, not all the rich still enjoyed their prewar wealth and were able to afford domestic staff. A way of life had passed. ∎

FAR LEFT: *Advertisement, 1911. Society women of the Belle Époque would not have been able to get dressed without the help of a maid.*

LEFT: *This 1928 black beaded evening dress, fur-trimmed coat and short slick hairstyle epitomize the new simplicity of the Roaring Twenties.*

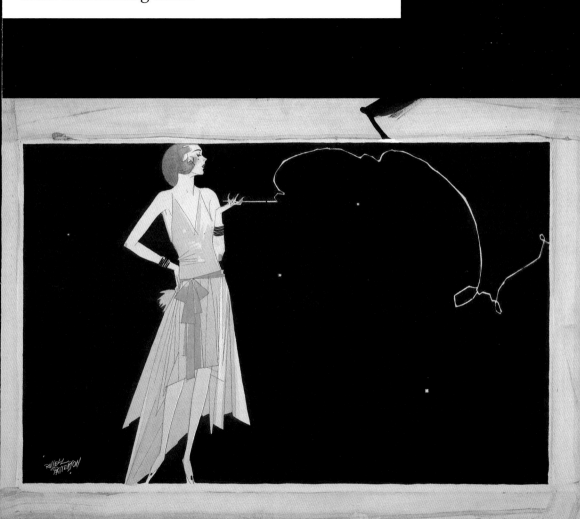

A 1920s flapper. Illustration by Russell Patterson.

Bronzed and beautiful

SUNBATHING

Brigitte Bardot in 1960, when she created a scandal by sunbathing topless in Saint-Tropez.

Until the end of the Victorian era, no self-respecting lady tolerated a suntan: a brown face and hands were indicative of the working classes, implying time spent at manual labour and physical work in the fields. Upper-class women took care to protect their fashionably pale complexions from the sun's rays with bonnets and parasols.

With the explosion of the craze for sunbathing in the 1920s came new fashions both on and off the beach, including revealing clothes that would show off a golden tan. In the early 1900s, doctors and scientists had begun actively to promote sun therapy for the benefits of vitamin D, which is produced by the skin when exposed to sunlight. The tide was already turning. Then, when the fashion designer Coco Chanel was spotted sporting a rich tan in the 1920s, her acolytes took note, and decided that they wanted a golden sun-kissed body too, ideally acquired on the French Riviera. By 1923, a December tan had become a status symbol, synonymous with the luxury of winter travel.

Fashion designers swiftly responded to the new craze. Jean Patou, Sonia Delaunay and Elsa Schiaparelli conjured up loud, attention-seeking swimming costumes whose bright colours emphasized a tan. The 1930s trend for halter-neck swimsuits allowed for a seamlessly golden-tanned back, which could then be displayed in a low-backed white slinky dress in the evening. The next decade brought with it informal beachwear that revealed the flesh – blouses showing the midriff, shorts and thong sandals.

The launch of **the bikini** in 1946 gave women an excuse to flaunt even more bare flesh. But in the 1960s Brigitte Bardot did the unthinkable and scandalously started sunbathing topless, at Saint-Tropez in the South of France. The designer Rudi Gernreich backed this celebration of semi-nudity by launching his monokini of 1964 – a pair of high-waisted bikini bottoms, held up only by long halter straps and completely revealing the breasts.

Today, topless or nude sunbathing is common (although nudist activities are not actively promoted by fashion houses). Bikinis are often tiny triangles of fabric, and swimsuits are sometimes slashed or pierced with large holes to reveal the flesh. Sunbathing, however, is hardly a health cure today, with excessive exposure to the sun known to cause premature ageing and, potentially, skin cancer. There is no going back to bonnets, parasols and darkened parlours at midday, but rather than baking in the sun, women are increasingly faking it with all-over spray-tans instead. ∎

au Lido.

At the Lido *by Georges Barbier,*
1924, an illustration of sunbathers

Girls take on the boys

TROUSERS FOR WOMEN

Coco Chanel borrows from the boys and wears yachting pants in 1910.

Walk down any city street in the West today, and you will see more women wearing trousers than skirts. Yet trousers for women did not become even remotely acceptable until as recently as the 1920s.

The legendary French actress Sarah Bernhardt daringly wore trousers on stage in the late nineteenth century, while early enthusiasts of bicycling favoured divided skirts for practical reasons.

Designer Paul Poiret took inspiration from the costumes of the Ballets Russes for his harem pants of 1909 – wide trousers gathered with a band at the ankle. And at the society beach resort of Deauville, Coco Chanel introduced elegant yachting pants, at first for herself and then for other women who admired her style. She explained: 'It was Deauville and I never liked to stay on the beach in my bathing costume, so I bought myself a pair of white sailor pants, and added a turban and ropes of jewels, and I must say, I looked like a maharani.' Women in the 1920s started to choose trousers as beachwear and loungewear, but only the very outrageous dared to wear them on the street.

The bisexual film star Marlene Dietrich, sometimes referred to as 'the best-dressed man in Hollywood', caused a scandal during the 1930s and '40s by wearing trouser suits as daywear. The Parisian chief of police considered her attire so shocking that he ordered her to leave the city.

During World War II it became acceptable for women to wear trousers for wartime work in the fields and the factories, but when peace resumed in 1945 they went back to their skirts and dresses. Trousers on women were still generally viewed as unnatural and unattractive. However, capri pants, bermuda shorts and tight trousers that laced up at the knee were still worn as leisurewear.

It was in the Swinging Sixties that women really started to embrace the comfort and practicality of menswear, wearing trousers for work and to parties. The practice still retained its shock value for some, and women wearing trousers were often refused entry to formal establishments, even restaurants. Yves Saint Laurent's 1966 sleek tailored trouser suit, known as Le Smoking, was controversial at first, but this would be the garment that eventually sealed the acceptability of trousers as an alternative to **the skirt suit** or dress. Here was a formal, elegant suit for the girls, acceptable to all. Women could finally wear the trousers and get the respect they deserved. ■

'Women wearing trousers were often refused entry to formal establishments'

The new artificial silk

IDEA Nº 19

RAYON

Rayon was one of the first man-made fibres to be used for clothing. 'Art silk', 'gloss' or 'fibre silk', as the fabric was first known, was soft and shiny, and was used as an alternative to silk, velvet, crêpe and linen. In 1924 the name was changed to rayon. It revolutionized the clothing market, as it was comfortable, economical to make and dyed well.

During the 1880s a Frenchman, Count Hilaire de Chardonnet, developed fabric made of cellulose after studying the silkworm, with a view to making a version of silk using chemicals. But the method for actually processing viscose rayon was invented by three British chemists, Charles Frederick Cross, Edward John Bevan and Clayton Beadle, and patented in 1892. The material is in fact produced from wood pulp, and so cannot be truly called a synthetic. The first reliable fabrics woven from viscose rayon filaments appeared between 1910 and 1914.

During the 1920s, manufacturers used rayon to make cheap dresses, linings, slips, knickers and stockings. With technological advances they could eliminate its artificial sheen, making it suitable for knitted fabric and more expensive daywear and evening wear. Thirties women on a budget bought slips and camiknickers made from lace-trimmed rayon instead of silk – perfect for the dark days of the Depression when money was tight. At the other end of the scale, high-end designers such as Elsa Schiaparelli experimented by blending rayon with natural fibres. Rayon was not resilient, but when combined with acetate it produced a stronger, more convenient fabric that retained its shape and was wrinkle-free, so eliminating the need for time-consuming ironing.

One of the benefits of rayon is that it can be controlled at the production stage, so that it can be made to imitate wool, silk, cotton or linen. It is still used for dresses, **sport**swear, skirts and suits, and is often found blended with other fibres. ■

A 1920s advertising poster promotes the benefits of rayon stockings.

'Thirties women on a budget bought slips
and camiknickers made from lace-trimmed
rayon instead of silk'

*High-end designers experimented
with the new fibre, using it as
an alternative to silk. This elegant
dress by Mary Black from 1950
is made from rayon-satin.*

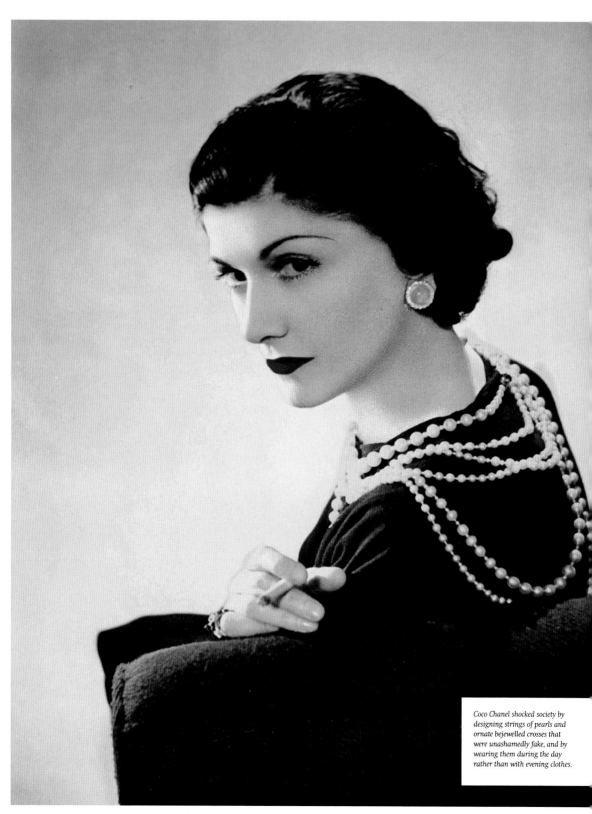

Coco Chanel shocked society by designing strings of pearls and ornate bejewelled crosses that were unashamedly fake, and by wearing them during the day rather than with evening clothes.

Flaunting great fakes

COSTUME JEWELLERY

The ancient Egyptians made beads of glass, and imitation pearls were worn in Europe as early as the fifteenth century. But the world of high fashion always shunned imitation jewellery as mediocre. This was all to change in the early twentieth century.

Paul Poiret first challenged the notion that 'faux' jewellery was unacceptable as an accompaniment to **couture**, and Coco Chanel and Elsa Schiaparelli were to make history with it.

Poiret was the first couturier boldly to use costume jewellery in his collections, and by 1913 his clients were happy to be seen flaunting his tassel pieces and his amber heart or stone Buddha pendants. Chanel then rocked the boat, coming up with imitation pearls the size of gulls' eggs, and gems in unnatural colours. Her attitude was, simply: Why not mix fake with real and keep everyone guessing? In her eyes jewels should be worn as fashion accessories, rather than as a demon-stration of wealth or ancestry. French *Vogue* commented in 1927: 'This synthetic fashion, which is one of the typical symptoms of our time, is not without finesse, and that so many things are artificial – silk, pearls, fur – does not cease to make them chic.'

Chanel had opened her jewellery workshops in 1924 and began to use handfuls of paste jewels and fake pearls, combined with real gems in bold settings. They proved irresistible. Chanel herself flouted convention by wearing strings of fake pearls, long ropes of gilt chains and glittering Maltese crosses, even during the day. Her 1930s chains, pearls and glass-gemstone jewellery were designed to accessorize the clean lines of her **sport**y daywear collections. Chanel had brought **the little black dress** into fashion, and it now made the perfect backdrop for showing off large pieces of diamanté jewellery. Referring to her Fine Jewellery collection of 1932, she said: 'I wanted to cover women with constellations.'

Elsa Schiaparelli also had great fun with her jewellery collections during the 1930s, using wit and humour to attract her clients. They could not wait to get their hands on her snake hatpins, roller-skate brooches, charm bracelets, pins of can-can legs, lantern brooches that lit up and even facial jewellery, such as spectacles without the glass. At last fashion jewellery could be truly playful. ∎

Macaw feather fan earrings by Shaun Leane for Alexander McQueen, Spring/Summer 2003.

The success of the hidden fastening

IDEA № 21

THE ZIP

The humble zipper, that neat little fastener that women around the globe use to do up their clothes quickly each morning, is something that we take for granted. Imagine the fuss, and the time wasted, if there were no alternative to fiddly hooks and eyes, ties, buttons and poppers.

Vivienne Westwood's iconic bondage trousers of 1977 used the zip as detailing.

The modern zip as we know it, with its moveable clasp and interlinking teeth, was developed in 1913 by a Swedish–American engineer named Gideon Sundback. However, zips only started to be incorporated into womenswear fashion as late as the 1930s. Prior to that they were principally used as fasteners on money belts, US Navy jackets, underwear and luggage.

It was Elsa Schiaparelli who broke with convention in the early 1930s and ostentatiously used a zip as a fashion statement on the pockets of a beach jacket. A few years later, in 1935, she went a step further, dyeing zips to match the fabric of her collection and using them as decorative elements on evening dresses and jackets. Schiaparelli wrote in her 1954 autobiography, *Shocking Life:* 'What upset the poor, breathless reporters most were the zips. Not only did they appear for the first time but in the most unexpected places, even on evening clothes. The whole collection was full of them. Astounded buyers bought and bought. They had come prepared for every kind of strange button. Indeed these had been the signature of the house. But they were not prepared for zips.'

Designer Charles James followed Schiaparelli's lead and took the zip to another level when he created his bias-cut spiral Taxi dresses in the 1930s. For these he used panels of fabric wrapped round and round the body, fastening together with long zips instead of seams. Similarly, 1960s designer Rudi Gernreich used zips with large O-ring sliders as decorative devices snaking round the body, as if the garment could be unzipped into narrow bands of fabric. Ossie Clark even designed raunchy jumpsuits for Mick Jagger's performances, which would unzip themselves on-stage. Vivienne Westwood played with zips for her notorious 1970s **punk** bondage trousers – drainpipes with zips, buckles, straps and a bum-flap of hanging fabric.

The zip's role today largely tends towards the mundane. It is used mainly as a convenient hidden fastening for dresses, tops, skirts, trousers, coats and boots – and, just sometimes, for the odd fashion statement. ■

48

'Subcultural movements have long been drawn to military clothes for their confrontational appearance'

Fashion enters the combat zone

MILITARY CLOTHING

When nations go to war, their citizens are exposed to more images of the military. And these influences inevitably creep into catwalk collections. Military clothing had a major impact on twentieth-century fashion, giving us such recognizable classics as pea jackets, aviator glasses and combat pants.

After World War I, womenswear adopted large patch pockets, braiding and frogging, and indeed the colour khaki. Thomas Burberry produced a civilian version of the raincoats worn by British Army officers, known as trench coats. The public also eagerly snapped up Ray-Ban aviator shades, which were launched to civilians in 1937, having been in use by US Army Air Corps pilots from the late 1920s.

World War II inspired designers to add practical detailing to their clothes, such as numerous pockets and thick leather belts. In the UK, all-in-one zip-up jumpsuits were designed for swiftly pulling over nightclothes in air raids; Winston Churchill famously wore his instead of a suit. Turbans and snoods, which were initially favoured for keeping workers' hair out of factory machines, became fashionable alternatives to hats.

Subcultural movements have long been drawn to military clothes, for their confrontational appearance as much as their practical qualities. The 1960s **mods** wore voluminous parkas, once worn by the US military, to protect their immaculate suits. **Hippies** also adopted the large coats, and adorned them with peace symbols. At the height of the Vietnam War, militant Black Power supporters and members of the anti-war movement wore multi-pocketed fatigue jackets as a form of protest. And **punk**s paraded the streets in **Dr. Martens boots** with combat trousers, often combined with long leather army coats.

More recently, the Gulf wars also freshly inspired designers to adopt military influences in the 1990s and 2000s. Combat-style clothing and camouflage prints in bright colours became a new street uniform, and combat trousers worked as an easy alternative to **jeans**.

In the world of fashion it seems that military styling, rather like war itself, just will not go away. ■

TOP: *Suits from 1945. The suit on the right has strong military detailing.*

ABOVE: *Sarah Jessica Parker wears combat pants in 2006.*

The celebration of simplicity

IDEA № 23

THE JUMPER

Coco Chanel wears an elegant jumper with trousers, c. 1930.

'With a black pullover and ten rows of pearls she revolutionized fashion,' was Christian Dior's verdict on Coco Chanel in *Talking About Fashion* (1954). Chanel's early sailor-blouse of around 1916 was a V-necked garment in cotton or silk that pulled over the head, and flowed over the hips.

Unusually for the time, it had no buttons or fastenings. She sold masculine-style jumpers for women, and adapted sweaters by slashing them down the front and trimming them with ribbons: they became best-sellers.

Before World War I broke out Chanel had opened her shop in Deauville, northern France, and introduced elegant clothing, much of it adapted from male dress, often customizing clothes from her lovers' wardrobes. She gave women comfort, elegance and the joy of dressing in clean lines and simple clothing. After the war, the jumper, or sweater, went on to form one of the keystones of the looks of the 1920s – it became a comfortable alternative to tailoring, often worn under a knitted cardigan with a simple skirt. By the 1930s knitted jumpers were starting to be worn as evening wear, glammed up with trimmings of chiffon, crêpe or sparkling jewel-encrusted embroidery.

The notorious sweater girls of the 1950s got pulses racing, as tight jumpers became popular with film actresses such as Lana Turner and Jane Russell. These sweaters emphasized the breasts, particularly when worn with a push-up-and-point bra, leaving little to the imagination. Teenagers of the 1950s swiftly adopted the look to their parents' horror and their boyfriends' delight. In the 1960s, the slimline skinny-rib jumper came into fashion. Mary Quant wrote in her autobiography:

'One day I pulled on an eight-year-old boy's sweater for fun. I was enchanted with the result. And, in six months, all the birds were wearing the skinny-ribs that resulted.'

Retailer and designer Joseph Ettedgui revolutionized the knitwear industry in the 1980s with his Joseph Tricot range, selling luxurious ribbed sloppy joe jumpers, and fine tightly knitted tops. With the demise of the tailored jacket during the 1990s, an elegant jumper became acceptable for evening wear. The best came in cashmere. A cashmere jumper is now viewed, like a well-cut pair of **jeans** or a little black dress, as a wardrobe essential. To fulfill the demand for simple luxury, affordable cashmere became available on the high street for the first time, with such stores as Primark and Marks & Spencer producing their own versions of the cashmere jumper.

Chanel had said: 'Simplicity is a very delicate thing, not to be confused with poverty. My luck was to have understood that luxury is inseparable from simplicity.' Once again she had helped to pioneer what would become one of the most basic fashion staples in any woman's wardrobe. ∎

*Sweater girls Marilyn Monroe
(left, in 1952) and Sophia Loren
(right, in 1955) wear tight
jumpers worn over conical bras
to flaunt their assets. Teenage
girls rushed to copy the look.*

'The focus of the face
 had to be a pair of childlike
 wide eyes'

Glass Tears *photographed by Man Ray in 1932.*

IDEA № 24

FALSE EYELASHES

Where would flirtatious brides and red-carpet beauties be today without their false eyelashes? Some of the first falsies were created in 1916 by the American film director D. W. Griffith for his leading lady, Seena Owen.

He wanted her lashes to be so long that they brushed her cheeks when she blinked. Griffith asked a wig-maker to attach some interwoven human hair to a fine piece of gauze, which was glued to her eyelids. The effect was extraordinary.

However, it was not until several decades later that false eyelashes really took off for the woman on the street. They became popular in the 1950s, and by the 1960s were a fashion essential. Lipstick was worn pale, meaning that the focus of the face had to be a pair of childlike wide eyes. The waiflike supermodel Twiggy often wore false eyelashes above and below her eyes, or sometimes attached to her bottom lashes alone. The model Jean Shrimpton and actresses Marianne Faithfull, Sophia Loren and Elizabeth Taylor were all renowned for their luscious lashes, and the singer Dusty Springfield became known for her 'panda-eyed' look.

The 1960s versions were made of bristle-like plastic: their staying power was limited, and they tended to fall off. Salvation came in the 2000s when the Japanese invented individual fake lashes that could be glued on to real eyelashes, one by one. These were like hair extensions for the eyes, lasting up to two months. Today false lashes are as popular as earrings and lipstick. Shu Uemura created a set of paper-clip style lashes with Dutch fashion designers Viktor & Rolf, and in 2009 the UK band Girls Aloud launched their own range of false lashes in collaboration with Eylure. Flirting has never looked so good. ■

Long lashes backstage before the John Galliano Autumn/Winter 2008 show.

Why Coco Chanel was the original material girl

ABOVE: *John Galliano poses with Princess Diana in 1996. She wears one of his slip dresses.*

BELOW: *John Galliano shows a seductive petticoat-inspired dress for Christian Dior in 1997.*

IDEA № 25

UNDERWEAR AS OUTERWEAR

Corsets, bustiers and slips bared in public were for a long time unimaginable, but nowadays they may even fail to be provocative. Chanel paved the way in 1916 by using beige knit jersey, traditionally used for mens' underwear, to make chic womenswear. It was scandalous but her clients loved it.

Far from minding, the fashionable ladies of Deauville and Biarritz positively snapped up Chanel's new designs. Couturier Jacques Fath made waves with his risqué evening dresses with corset lacing in the 1940s, but it was the ever-provocative designer Vivienne Westwood who really changed fashion by offering underwear as outerwear. In the late 1970s, **punk**s strutted the streets of London in rubber negligées and stockings, bought from Westwood and Malcolm McLaren's shop SEX. This was underwear worn as outerwear largely for its shock value.

The 1980s was the decade when underwear as outerwear made it to the mainstream. The image of Madonna dancing on-stage during her 1990 Blond Ambition tour wearing a Jean Paul Gaultier corset with a sharply pointed bra is unforgettable – but not scandalous. Madonna regularly performed in bras, slips and corsets. Jean Paul Gaultier offered corsets to wear with evening suits, and Westwood introduced satin bras layered over sweatshirts and dresses in 1982. When Westwood produced neo-Victorian short crinolines in 1985, she was ridiculed at first – and then, inevitably, other designers started copying the look. A Westwood corset top became highly desirable as evening wear, not least because it enhanced the cleavage magnificently.

During the 1990s, bejewelled thongs were worn to ride up above low-slung **jeans**. Women danced, partied and even got married in tiny slips of bias-cut silk, and camisoles with slim spaghetti straps or lace detailing. The master of these petticoat evening dresses or slip dresses, as they became known, was John Galliano. He famously managed to coax Princess Diana into one, and images of the People's Princess in her risqué petticoat made headlines around the world.

More recently, in 2009 Dolce & Gabbana produced a show-stopping tulle corset dress with sexy criss-cross lacing snaking up the sides of the body, demonstrating that underwear details that just hint at provocation are perhaps the most enticing of all. ∎

'Madonna performed in bras,
slips and corsets'

Madonna struts her stuff in
Jean Paul Gaultier corsetry for
her Blond Ambition tour, 1990.

Sleek lines for a modern world

THE CLUTCH BAG

Embroidered clutch by Hilde Wagner-Ascher, 1925.

At the turn of the twentieth century, a society lady would never be seen carrying her own handbag. Anything except the tiniest purse was given to a man or a maid to hold. All this was to alter as women grew more independent and their changing lifestyles required that keys, money and make-up be instantly available at their fingertips.

The clutch bag, or 'pochette', evolved between 1916 and 1920. With its streamlined shape and snap-jaw fastenings, it mirrored the modern, no-frills aesthetic of the 1920s. The architect and designer Le Corbusier enthused: 'The luxury item is well made, clean of line, pure and strong, revealing its quality in its very spareness.' In the early 1920s the style leader Coco Chanel produced clutch bags in leather or Bakelite or in fabrics matching her garments. Other designers, including Edward Molyneux, launched their own versions of the slimline bag. Sonia Delaunay and the jeweller Jean Fouquet introduced graphically ornate clutches in bold colours.

During the 1920s and 1930s, few fashionable women were seen without a clutch. It was the most popular bag of the era. As the shape was so simple, designers experimented with the bag's colour, texture and embellishment – snakeskin, lizardskin, shagreen and patent leather, with dramatic rhinestones and gold braid for evening. Designers used Bakelite and Perspex, the new modern materials, and simpler bags were embossed or embroidered. While sun-ray designs and Art Deco and Egyptian motifs were fashionable during the 1920s, designs of the 1930s focused more on exotic reptile skins and sparkling diamanté fastenings.

During World War II, women in Europe shunned the clutch for larger, more practical bags that would hold essentials while they were bicycling, doing war work or during air raids. However, clutch bags have remained popular since then in their different guises: long and slim in the 1960s, soft and pliable in the 1970s and quilted in the 1980s. In the 2000s they were ludicrously large, so that by 2008 the offerings from Céline, Louis Vuitton and Fendi looked more like embellished art portfolios than bags, owing to their size. Perhaps it was time again for the men to carry a woman's bag of tricks and prove that chivalry was not quite dead. ■

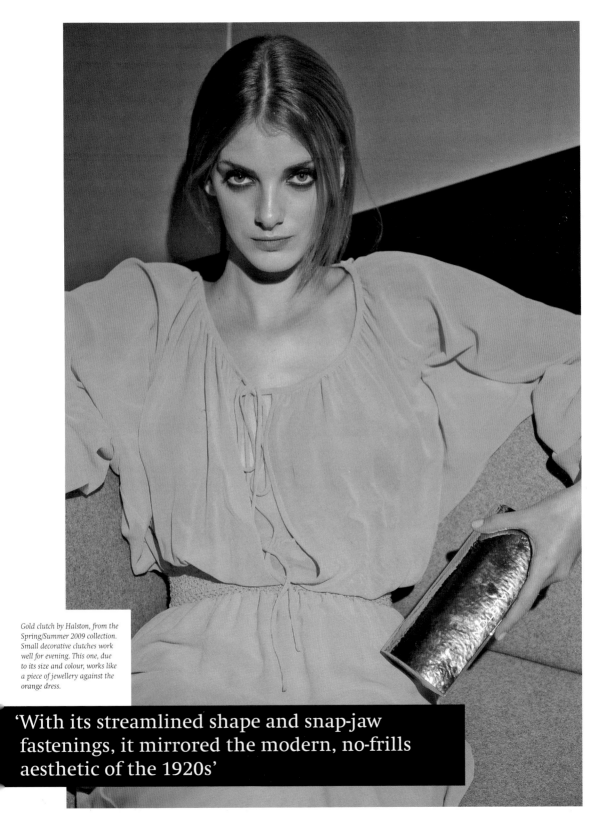

Gold clutch by Halston, from the Spring/Summer 2009 collection. Small decorative clutches work well for evening. This one, due to its size and colour, works like a piece of jewellery against the orange dress.

'With its streamlined shape and snap-jaw fastenings, it mirrored the modern, no-frills aesthetic of the 1920s'

The timekeeping essential

IDEA № 27
THE WRISTWATCH

The first wristwatches were small clock faces attached to ladies' bracelets as ornaments, and were worn at the end of the nineteenth century. It was not until after World War I that wristwatches were in demand for both sexes.

When Rolex entrepreneur Hans Wilsdorf started to promote the wristwatch as the essential timepiece, male critics said that they would rather wear a skirt than a wristwatch, and stuck to their gold pocket watches on chains. However, for pilots and artillery officers fighting in World War I, the wristwatch was the only sensible solution to timekeeping. Expandable bracelets attached the clockface to the wrist, and pierced metal 'shrapnel guards' covered the glass. The soldiers brought home these 'trench watches' as souvenirs, and wristwatches finally became acceptable for men too. In 1914 Rolex was awarded a precision certificate by Britain's Kew Observatory (an endorsement previously bestowed only on marine chronometers), proving wrong those who criticized the accuracy of wristwatches. By the 1930s, the wristwatch had overtaken the pocket watch as the most desirable mobile timekeeping device.

New innovations started to drive watch design. The compact quartz timekeeping mechanisms first launched in 1969 meant that absolute accuracy could be achieved and marketed economically, while the digital displays of the 1970s inspired more functional design. In 1983 the Swatch watch company launched inexpensive, fashion-led designs in brightly coloured plastic, with highly efficient and compact inner workings. They were an instant hit.

Just as they did with **sunglasses** and handbags, designer brands such as Louis Vuitton, Gucci and Chanel started to include luxury branded wristwatches in their ranges. By 2000 the mobile phone was beginning to replace the watch as the most popular method of telling the time. But then Samsung, and later Apple, launched their smart watches, which were, essentially, watches, computers and mobile phones all squeezed into a tiny wrist-size bracelet. For the younger generation traditional watches became less popular as functional items. This meant that a watch had to do something else as well as tell the time – such as double up as an elegant piece of jewellery. Marc Jacobs launched a series of watches on necklace chains using cherry or zipper motifs, brands such as Calvin Klein and DKNY produced pretty watches strung on charm bracelets, while other designers set watches into rings. Fashion had gone full circle in 100 years, with women desiring watches as jewellery once more. ∎

ABOVE: *Marc by Marc Jacobs pendant watch, 2009.*

BELOW: *A striking alternative to a wristwatch, this 'Nougat' ring by Dior, 2004, is made from white gold with pink mother of pearl.*

Buccellati watch with engraved silver face and gold leaf motif bracelet strap, 1930s.

'They were perfect for showing off the nubile figures of film starlets'

Fluid bias-cut dress, 1944. Bias-cut dresses allowed the fabric to move and flow with the body.

Cutting at an angle to create curves

THE BIAS CUT

When fabric is cut on the bias, it is cut diagonally across the direction of the weave, so that the warp and weft (the 'grain' of the fabric) fall diagonally over the figure rather than horizontally and vertically.

Material cut in this way is naturally elastic, a property that can be used to make dresses cling and stretch on contact with the body's curves, producing an elegant effect and flattering the figure.

The French dressmaker Madeleine Vionnet, who opened her Paris fashion house in 1912, is known as the mistress of the bias cut. Until her ingenious ideas began to influence fashion in the 1920s, the bias cut had been used in the twentieth century principally for collars. Unusually, Vionnet designed her dresses by draping, gathering and twisting fabric on a small wooden dummy rather than using traditional pattern-cutting techniques. Many of her dresses had no fastenings, and pulled straight over the head – it was only when a body filled them that they magically came to life. Vionnet was one of the pioneers in rejecting the corset. She focused on achieving a figure-hugging fit with dresses that flowed smoothly over the body in one layer of fabric – they incorporated no under-dress. They were often long with halter or cowl necks, and sweeping low backs. She favoured lightweight crêpe, gabardine and satin, which were pliable and draped easily.

Bias-cut dresses reached the height of their popularity in the late 1920s and the 1930s. They were perfect for showing off the nubile figures of film starlets, and many of the slinky Hollywood gowns typical of the period were cut on the bias. Madame Grès, who opened her Paris house in 1934, also became famed for her bias-cut dresses and classical drapery inspired by ancient Greece. She took wool, silk and jersey and draped them into clever dresses, which looked simple on the body but had a masterly intricacy of design.

Vionnet's innovation has continued to provide inspiration for later designers. During the 1980s Azzedine Alaïa employed this cutting method for his skin-skimming dresses, and today's John Galliano and Zac Posen are both celebrated for reworking the bias cut into their own designs. 'The whole idea of cutting on the bias was brilliant,' said Galliano on the subject. 'It was elastic before there was elastic.' ∎

TOP: *John Galliano for Christian Dior combines a structured bodice with a figure-skimming bias-cut skirt for this white dress for Autumn/Winter 2007.*

ABOVE: *Dress by Madeleine Vionnet, 1938. The mistress of the bias cut, Vionnet revolutionized fashion with her draped and fluid dress designs.*

Fashion gets fit and fabulous

IDEA № 29
SPORT

Sportswear played a central role in twentieth-century fashion, changing and driving clothing in a way no one could have anticipated. It altered the way women dress, move and feel in their clothes. Fashion and sportswear are irreversibly intertwined, and designers working in each field borrow ideas from the other.

Sports dress has crossed over to become acceptable daywear, inspiring women to dress more casually and comfortably. Today fashion designers draw on elements initially developed for sport; while sportswear itself is stylish as well as functional.

In post-World War I Europe the demise of the lace-up corset meant that women had to work hard to achieve the new lithe silhouette that fashion demanded. To be slim in the 1920s was essential. For their sporting activities women needed the appropriate skiwear, swimming costumes, skating clothes and tennis whites, and the sporting look became fashionable in itself.

Jean Patou and Coco Chanel were already designing daywear that was sportier and more boyish than ever before – simple, pared-down clothes, more practical and suitable for the increasingly independent woman. Patou adapted some elements of sportswear for his fashion lines. In 1925 he opened a sportswear store, Coin des Sports, and he designed the match outfits for the French tennis star Suzanne Lenglen – short dresses and headbands. They became instantly

fashionable. Chanel produced sleek sporty womenswear in cotton jersey, and introduced men's yachting trousers to her clients.

But the roots of modern sportswear, or casualwear, really lie in the United States. With the boom in **mass-manufacturing** after 1939, American women adopted a more casual style. They took to wearing comfortable and practical separates. And rather than following the latest fashion fads laid down by Paris **couture**, they looked to their own ready-to-wear designers, such as Claire McCardell. This tendency was to influence the way women dressed around the world. By the 1950s, American teenagers were wearing easy separates and **trainers** as casualwear.

From the 1970s onwards, there was a constant crossover from the gym and the court to the street. Aerobics brought disco-style **Lycra** leggings and leotards, while jogging and skating introduced shorts, legwarmers and headbands. American designer Norma Kamali raised the humble tracksuit to high fashion, with ra-ra skirts, leggings and cotton fleece tops. And in the cities, kids dressed like their favourite sports

stars, from basketball heroes in the 1970s to skateboarders in the 1990s.

Powerful sports brands were keenly aware of the influence of sports stars, and called in big-name players to endorse their products and boost sales, notably Michael Jordan for Nike and David Beckham for Adidas.

Fashion designers looked at new sports fabric technology to gain inspiration for their designs. They launched their own sports label spin-offs in the 1990s – among them Prada Sport, DKNY Active and Polo Sport. Meanwhile, other partnerships with sports brands were struck up for specific ranges of clothing or trainers – Yohji Yamamoto worked with Adidas, Alexander McQueen with Puma and Commes des Garçons with Speedo. High fashion had never looked so fit and fabulous. ■

BELOW: *Collection for Adidas by Stella McCartney for Spring/Summer 2009.*

RIGHT: *Tennis star Suzanne Lenglen wears whites by Jean Patou in 1926. She started a trend for headbands and sleek, sporty dresses.*

N°5

N°5
CHANEL
PARIS

PARFUM

The world's most famous fragrance

IDEA № 30

CHANEL NO. 5

When Marilyn Monroe was asked what she wore in bed, she famously quipped: 'Why, Chanel No. 5, of course.' This distinguished scent, in its iconic bottle, is one of the most successful in history, worn by millions of women since it was launched in the 1920s. Still in production today, it changed fashion-house fragrances forever.

Chemical advances in the nineteenth century meant that perfumiers started to incorporate synthetic ingredients into scent, particularly in place of an expensive or rare natural ingredient. Synthetic components also made a fragrance last longer on the skin. But Coco Chanel turned the perfume industry on its head when in 1921, with her perfumier Ernest Beaux, she launched a perfume that *deliberately* smelt artificial – Chanel No. 5.

Until then, perfume was made to smell like flowers – jasmine, rose, lily of the valley – and came trussed in feminine bottles. Chanel had wanted a scent that reminded her of the soap she used as a child. The resulting fragrance had no recognizable floral scent, came in a bold medicinal-style bottle and looked clean and modern. Just as she celebrated **costume jewellery**, Chanel revelled in the scent's artificiality. Chanel No. 5 contained more than 80 different ingredients, and mixed numerous natural floral scents with synthetic ingredients. Radically for the time, its top note – what you first smell when the scent hits the skin – was created using floral aldehydes (powerful synthetic molecules that intensify aromatic scents).

In 1911, Paul Poiret had launched his own perfume range, Les Parfums de Rosine, named after his oldest daughter. He linked each fragrance to a gown he had designed, and used both chemical and natural ingredients. But he missed a marketing opportunity to brand it with the name of his fashion house. Chanel did not. Her scent bore her name. The House of Worth, Edward Molyneux and Elsa Schiaparelli quickly followed suit with their own branded fragrances, and Christian Dior had a 1947 hit with the successful Miss Dior.

Cheap international travel and duty-free shopping meant that women of all classes were able to buy fashion-house fragrances during the 1960s. Twenty years later the fashion brands were aggressively marketing their house scents with moving-image and still advertising campaigns, all clamouring to corner a segment of this lucrative market. Erotic imagery boosted sales, led by Calvin Klein's raunchy ads for Obsession. By the 1990s, Klein had made history again by setting a trend for unisex scent with his fragrance CK One. New perfume trends come and go but without the innovation of Chanel No. 5, we might all still have been smelling of roses or lavender. ∎

ABOVE: *Silkscreen prints by Andy Warhol of Chanel No. 5 (1985), used for the advertising campaign in 1997.*

OPPOSITE PAGE: *Actress Audrey Tatou features in an advertisement for Chanel No. 5 in 2009.*

Bow lips and smoky eyes

PAINTED LADIES

Cosmetics have been used for centuries, even millennia – the ancient Egyptians used kohl to emphasize their eyes as long as 6,000 years ago. But at the start of the twentieth century, the look for high-class ladies was pale, natural and demure. Their hair might be lavishly rolled and pinned up, but obvious make-up, painted nails and dyed hair were eschewed as vulgar.

By the 1920s the natural look was no longer fashionable. Artifice was all, as demonstrated by the 'Sisters G' in Berlin in 1925.

The 1920s were to introduce a new notion of beauty that could be achieved by artifice – short hair and a painted face. Quite suddenly, a woman would not be seen dead on the street without her lips painted into a cupid bow, her eyes defined with kohl and mascara and her complexion smoothed out with make-up. Flappers plucked and pencilled in their eyebrows, and coloured their nails. Elaborate hair was transformed with scissors into a boyish bob or Eton crop, and a high level of obvious grooming became fashionable and smart for the bright young things.

Virginia Woolf wrote in her 1925 novel *Mrs Dalloway*: 'To his eye the fashions had never been so becoming; the long black cloaks; the slimness; the elegance; and then the delicious and apparently universal habit of paint. Every woman, even the most respectable, had roses blooming under glass; lips cut with a knife; curls of Indian ink.'

Both the cool cats of Swinging London in the 1960s and the **punk**s of the following decade would appropriate this appreciation of artifice. During the 1960s, the popular look was childlike and boyish – a pale made-up face framed by short hair snipped into a Vidal Sassoon crop – and was famously promoted by Mary Quant and the model Twiggy. Teamed with heavy black eyeliner, elaborately curled lashes and pale lipstick, the emphasis was on making women look like large-eyed dolls.

The punks particularly enjoyed playing with hair and make-up, and accentuated the shock factor, cutting off their hair or teasing it up into dramatic spikes of lurid colours. Faces were covered with white make-up, and black-rimmed eyes and dark lipstick were complemented by shiny black nails. Artifice was all: these girls were never going to wear flowers in their hair as the **hippies** once did. ∎

BELOW: *Twiggy, 1967. In the 1960s make-up focused on the eyes, and women emulated Twiggy's wide-eyed doll-like style.*

RIGHT: *A London punk, 1977. Punk make-up was shockingly bold, with black lips and nails.*

TOP LEFT: *Red sandals by Yves Saint Laurent, 2010.*

TOP RIGHT: *Black wedges by Salvatore Ferragamo, 1940.*

MIDDLE LEFT: *Black flat sandals by Valentino, 2010.*

MIDDLE CENTRE: *Pink flip-flops.*

MIDDLE RIGHT: *Black stilettos by Pucci, Spring/Summer 2010.*

BOTTOM LEFT: *Blue cutaway ankle boots by Sergio Rossi, Spring/Summer 2011.*

BOTTOM CENTRE: *Black heels with a flesh-tone trim by Yves Saint Laurent, Spring/Summer 2010.*

BOTTOM RIGHT: *Platform sandal by Salvatore Ferragamo, 1938.*

Daring to flaunt the feet

IDEA № 32
THE OPEN SHOE

Sandals are the most primitive shoes in human history. The ancient Egyptians, Greeks and Romans found them ideal for protecting the soles of their feet, and the simple yet practical design was standard for many centuries before more sophisticated shoes were developed.

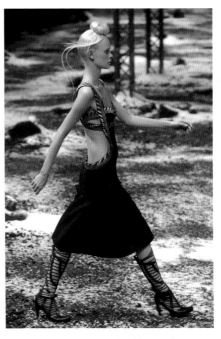

A model steps out in cutaway boots at the Alexander McQueen Autumn/Winter 2003 show.

Their acceptance in twentieth-century fashion was, however, gradual. Sandals first came into fashion during the 1920s. As the French Riviera became the favoured summer destination for the upper classes, women started to feel more confident about showing naked skin in public. André Perugia made opulent high-heeled sandals in suede and snakeskin for the evening, while the Italian Salvatore Ferragamo introduced the sandal to America. Although peep-toes, slingbacks and sandals were available for day and evening by the end of the 1930s, some women still regarded them as taboo away from the beach. Respectable women had covered their feet in the past and, even in 1939, the style arbiters at *Vogue* deemed that sandals were too revealing to be worn on the street. The slingback, the design of which suggested the exposure of the rear, was seen as risqué. It was not until after World War II that it became fully acceptable to expose the insteps, heels and toes in public.

Pretty, opulent Italian sandals complemented **the New Look** fashions of the 1950s, while American designer Beth Levine pioneered flat-heeled sandals in clear acrylic. The 1970s brought a renewed enthusiasm for peep-toes reminiscent of the 1940s, as well as larger-than-life platform sandals. By the 1990s and 2000s, elegant strappy sandals had come back into fashion, with designers such as Manolo Blahnik and Jimmy Choo catering for stars and starlets, who loved the height and the delicacy – and probably the sexual connotations – of walking high above the ground on nearly-naked feet. On the street, sophisticated and ornamented versions of the flip-flop (particularly Brazilian Havaianas) and chunky Birkenstock sandals became *de rigueur* for summer casualwear.

In 2007 and 2008 gladiator sandals hit the catwalk and the streets. Some had lacing that snaked up the ankle to the knee, while others sported vertiginous heels. Two thousand years after its origins, Roman fashion was once more back in town. ■

IDEA № 33
THE LITTLE BLACK DRESS

Black crêpe dress with embroidered skirt by Chanel, 1926.

Sleek, black and simple, the little black dress is an essential fashion staple. The hemline hovers around the knee (it is never long), but the sleeve and neck detailing, as well as the fabric, change with the ebb and flow of fashion. However, its essence is in its versatility.

The LBD can be worn for the office, for cocktail parties and for dinners, and, like a white shirt or a pair of **jeans**, it is a true fashion classic whose popularity spans the decades. Yet this simple, understated wardrobe essential was once deemed unfit for a lady. Pale colours were more difficult to clean, and therefore were associated with status and wealth. Black was the opposite, and black dresses were worn by women in service. No rich woman wanted to dress like her maid.

When a black dress was worn by a lady, it signified mourning, and black would never have been chosen as a fashion colour. The fallen soldiers of World War I left behind them vast armies of mourning widows, sisters and mothers. Society became very used to seeing women of all classes clad in black outside the house, including many young widows.

Then Coco Chanel came along and changed the rules. To great fanfare, American *Vogue* first featured her sleek black dress in 1926. With its short skirt, long sleeves and diagonal detailing it looked new, streamlined and modern – perfect for the 1920s forward-thinking woman. *Vogue* even likened its simplicity of form to the model-T Ford. Once again Chanel had neatly taken the class values out of clothing. The little black dress could make any woman look elegant, and without great expense. It became a uniform, often made of velvet and lace for the evening, and wool for the day.

'You can wear black at any hour of the day or night, at any age and for any occasion,' said Christian Dior. 'A little black dress is the most essential thing in any woman's wardrobe.'

Fashion doyenne Wallis Simpson, later the Duchess of Windsor, agreed: 'When a little black dress is right, there is nothing else to wear in its place.'

And which woman today does not have a black dress in her wardrobe? From Prada to Preen to Calvin Klein, almost all designers offer some version of this fashion classic. It slims the figure; it is a fine backdrop for jewellery; it flatters blond hair. It can be worn for party after party and thanks to its anonymous colouring, does not run the risk of being remembered on future occasions. It is hard to imagine a time when an LBD will not still look modern and elegant. ∎

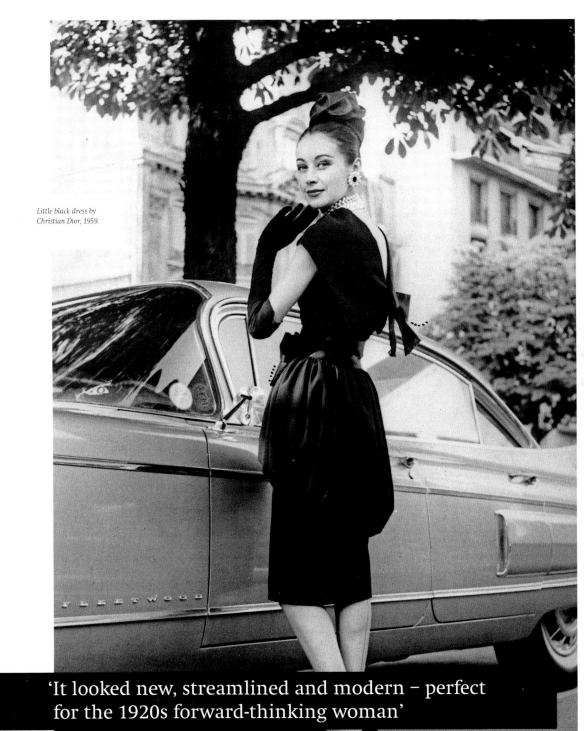

Little black dress by Christian Dior, 1959.

'It looked new, streamlined and modern – perfect for the 1920s forward-thinking woman'

A naked Sophie Dahl strikes
a provocative pose in this
advertisement for the Yves Saint
Laurent fragrance Opium, 2000.
Photograph by Steven Meisel.

OPIUM
le parfum par
YVESSAINTLAURENT

Letting it all hang out

IDEA № 34
PUBLIC NUDITY

Daringly low-cut dresses from the latter 1920s reveal the skin, a leap forward from the 1900s, when it was shocking to show an ankle in public.

In 1900 it was considered risqué for a respectable woman even to show her ankles in public. Yet that same woman's grandchildren, once grown-up, would be able to sunbathe topless or even naked on a public beach.

In the West, the twentieth century saw an extraordinary revolution in public attitudes to nudity, which swung from one extreme to the other. In fashion, as revealing more flesh became acceptable, so designers were able to experiment with ever-skimpier styles.

During World War I, skirts crept above a woman's ankle for practical reasons – bomb shelters and munitions factories were no places for sweeping dresses. The bright young things of the 1920s dared to reveal their knees and even a flash of stocking top, in their new short flapper dresses. During the 1930s, armless body-skimming dresses with daringly low backs showed even more flesh, and designer Madeleine Vionnet produced a bold evening dress that exposed the midriff.

Interestingly, sandals were still seen only as beachwear, as even adventurous women would still not reveal their naked feet. When Louis Réard launched his prototype bikini in 1946, he encountered a major problem: his models refused to wear it. He had to hire a stripper to model his new design to the public. But times were changing fast. By the 1960s Brigitte Bardot was **sunbathing** topless in Saint-Tropez; and other sun worshippers soon followed her lead, though perhaps delighting the onlookers less.

With the contraceptive pill available in the United States and Europe by the early 1960s, a new era of sexual permissiveness and liberation was born. The **hippies** gleefully embraced nudity and indulged in far greater sexual liberty than previous generations. Fashion reflected this in miniskirts reaching buttock-skimming heights, and these in turn gave way to the craze for **hot pants** in the 1970s. The desire to show naked flesh continued unabated, with G-strings and low-cut, pubic-hair-skimming hipster **jeans** becoming popular in the 1990s.

After the turn of the century the label Imitation of Christ launched a collection with topless models in microshorts pushing vacuum cleaners. When Sophie Dahl modelled naked in a sexually provocative manner for the Yves Saint Laurent Opium campaign in 2000, shot by Steven Meisel, the posters were banned by the British Advertising Standards Agency after more than 700 complaints. But this was tame compared with the soft porn images used for the Tom Ford men's fragrance ad in 2007, in which a bottle of perfume was photo-graphed between the spread legs of a nude model, her fingers resting gently on the bottle top. To previous generations it would have been unthinkably obscene. Today, it is just advertising. ∎

Borrowing from the boys

BELOW: *Singer Ciara shows the strikingly androgynous effect of the trouser suit for women in 2004.*

BOTTOM: *Bianca Jagger cuts a dash at New York club Studio 54 in 1978 in sharply tailored black jacket, black trousers and white shirt.*

IDEA № 35
ANDROGYNY

Fashion regularly swings between celebrating voluptuous, womanly curves and favouring a more boyish silhouette. The flappers of the 1920s epitomized the lithe, androgynous look, as did the more recent skinny waif models of the 1990s, whose style was condemned by critics as 'heroin chic'.

The first time that this boyish look came into fashion in the twentieth century was during the 1920s. It was a decadent time for survivors of both the war and the great flu pandemic of 1918. The ratio of young women to men left was about three to one. Some girls were simply never going to find a man, so why should they not enjoy life with a male kind of freedom – easy-to-wear clothes and hairstyles, a job, cigarettes, cocktails, sex and dancing all night? That is, if you were rich enough.

Coco Chanel and Jean Patou both pioneered the androgynous look. Borrowing from the boys, Chanel produced blazers, pyjamas, reefer jackets, open-necked shirts worn with cufflinks, and jumpers for women. The bachelor girls, as these 1920s liberated women became known, strapped down their breasts, cut their hair short into shingles or Eton crops, masked their hips with dropped waistlines and revealed their legs with daringly short dresses. They were nicknamed *garçonnes* after Victor Margueritte's censored 1922 novel *La Garçonne* – a romp of career girls cutting off their hair and sleeping around. Yet in real life they were not the majority. The look made no real impact until 1926, and even then it was for the glamorous and elite. But its effect slowly filtered down, and for a while modern women took up a masculine style and smoked, drank and ditched their chaperones.

The 1960s ushered in another era that celebrated and almost worshipped youth. The Twiggy silhouette was sexless and childlike – skinny, with a big head and oversized eyes, and a tiny frame on which to hang wide clothes that hardly touched the body.

In the 1970s, as second-wave feminism gathered momentum, the gender distinction between fashions for young people grew increasingly blurred. Both sexes grew their hair and wore T-shirts, **jeans** and beads – while glam-rock stars David Bowie and Marc Bolan dressed up like showgirls, as did their fans. At last Yves Saint Laurent's Le Smoking trouser suit for women became acceptable.

Streetwear and workwear of the mid-1980s allowed men and women to adopt a similar unisex style, and today women have a choice. They can dress up in heels and dresses and flaunt their womanhood one day, and go for androgynous casualwear or a sleek trouser suit the next, and no one will think to comment. ∎

Coco Chanel models her own designs in the 1930s. Her success as an innovator was built upon adapting traditional masculine clothing for the 20th-century woman.

'Modern women took up a masculine style and smoked, drank and ditched their chaperones'

The hands-free solution

IDEA Nº 36

THE SHOULDER BAG

An independent urban woman, who needs to keep both hands free and her valuables safe, would be lost without her shoulder bag. A handbag with a strap that either hooks over one shoulder or is slung diagonally across the chest is far more practical than the strapless clutch bag, which is easy to lose and perfect for prowling muggers to snatch.

Elsa Schiaparelli had designed functional bags with shoulder straps as early as the 1930s. The benefits of the shoulder bag became obvious during World War II, when practicality was paramount. Hands could be kept unencumbered for more important tasks, while the bags could hold a gas mask as well as match an outfit.

After the war, European women wanted to leave the memories of practical austerity behind, and enjoyed the decadence of prettier, short-handled bags. But they still used the shoulder bag for country pursuits, in the summer and as a casualwear accessory. In the United States the shoulder bag stayed in fashion.

In 1955 Chanel introduced the much-copied quilted leather 2.55 shoulder bag, with its long gold chain strap (she used similar chains to weight the inside hems of her jackets). Other designers copied it, creating their own small bags strung on long straps.

During the 1960s the shoulder bag enjoyed a resurgence, accessorizing the new get-up-and-go youthful fashions of Swinging London; later the **hippies** carried large patchwork or embroidered carpet shoulder bags. As they in turn grew up and moved on, less flamboyant bags were in demand – either in soft leather and fitted with zips and integral straps, or practical satchel styles.

Prada's **nylon** rucksack of 1985 paved the way for light, **sport**y carryall bags for the girl about town, but by the turn of the century the rucksack had fallen from favour and sleeker bags were once again in demand. Fendi came up with one solution, designing a sleek compact bag with a short removable strap. It could be strung up over the shoulder and tucked under the arm, or carried strapless as a clutch. It was christened La Baguette.

Whether long or short, detachable or permanent, the shoulder strap had become a truly integral part of a woman's handbag. ■

ABOVE: *Wartime belles make full use of the practical straps on the new handbags in Paris in 1942, leaving their hands free for bicycling.*

BELOW: *Big and bold bag by Versace for Autumn/Winter 2008.*

Paris Hilton keeps her Fendi bag strapped close to her in 2006.

Shady ladies

IDEA № 37

SUNGLASSES

The Roman emperor Nero allegedly used polished emeralds to shade his eyes from the sun when watching the gladiatorial games. And although modern celebrity decadence might not go quite so far, where would today's paparazzi-shy celebrity be without her ubiquitous pair of shades?

Jackie Kennedy Onassis wears her signature large shades in 1968.

Lightly tinted corrective glasses were available during the nineteenth century for those with poor eyesight. But when in 1929 Sam Foster started to sell his Foster Grant sunglasses on the boardwalk in Atlantic City to the public, he started a revolution in eyewear. Not long afterwards, Bausch & Lomb launched their Ray-Ban aviator shades with anti-glare lenses, based on the green goggles the company supplied to the US Army Air Corps. They were the perfect solution for Hollywood starlets, who revelled in flash-bulb publicity, but wished to hide their eyes behind a layer of tinted glass. Women who in a previous age would have hidden behind a fan, could now smoulder mysteriously behind dark glasses.

The market grew rapidly during the 1930s, and sunglasses quickly became an essential fashion accessory, spurred on by images of movie stars in dark glasses in magazines and on the screen. Branded shades started to become more commonplace during the 1960s, and today a multinational fashion brand is incomplete without its own range of shades, alongside fragrances, jewellery and handbags.

Trends in sunglasses continually evolve. In the 1950s cat-eye sunglasses often had an upward flick. Small round glasses, as famously worn by John Lennon, were popular with **hippies** during the 1960s, but more stylish were **Space Age** white plastic opaque glasses by André Courrèges, perforated with a single horizontal slit for viewing the outside world. Frames grew to outsize proportions in the 1970s, as frequently seen on former First Lady Jacqueline Kennedy Onassis and singer Elton John. But by the 1980s and early 1990s the large rounded shades had been replaced by dramatically angular frames and dark lenses epitomized by the Ray-Ban Wayfarer. In 2000 designer Stella McCartney revived aviator-style shades. She decorated them with a small rhinestone heart, and they became one of the most sought-after accessories of the year. ∎

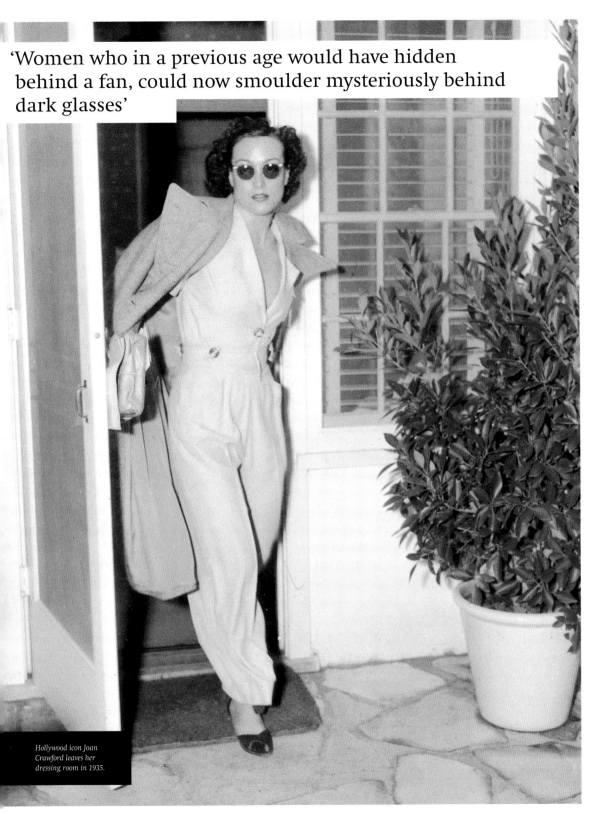

'Women who in a previous age would have hidden behind a fan, could now smoulder mysteriously behind dark glasses'

Hollywood icon Joan Crawford leaves her dressing room in 1935.

'Power-dressing became popular with ambitious working women seeking to make an impact in a man's world'

Wearing it like a man

IDEA № 38

THE SHOULDER PAD

Before the 1930s wide shoulder pads were exclusively for the use of men. But in 1931 the radical designer Elsa Schiaparelli designed the first wide-shouldered suit for women and everything changed.

The suit caused quite a stir. Hollywood studios took note, speedily appropriating it for such stars as Marlene Dietrich. With Joan Crawford's costumes for the 1932 film *Letty Lynton* helping to popularize the look, the trend for wide shoulders was sealed.

Elsa Schiaparelli wrote in her 1954 autobiography, *Shocking Life*: 'In Hollywood, one special item of popularity had preceded me – that of the padded shoulders. I had started them to give women a slimmer waist. They proved the Mecca of the manufacturers. Joan Crawford had adopted them and moulded her silhouette on them for years to come.' Sharp suits with squared-off padded shoulders were to take women through the 1930s and into the war years, until Dior revolutionized fashion with his New Look in 1947.

Shoulder pads came back into favour again, later in the century, with heavy-shouldered powersuits for women in the 1980s. Thierry Mugler and Claude Montana made some of the most extreme designs of this period. Power-dressing became popular with ambitious working women seeking to make an impact in a man's world, their top-heavy suits either imitating or challenging the broad-shouldered outline of the male torso.

By 2009, thanks to a legendary collection by Christophe Decarnin for Balmain, the neat little shoulder pad returned. This time round it was not wide, strong and manly, but feminine, with upturned pagoda shoulders and slim sleeves. 'They reflect a need for protection in this time of financial turmoil and, I must say, I personally find nothing gives a greater sense of security against encroaching bankruptcy than sinking my head between some giant boulders on my shoulders,' wrote *The Guardian*'s fashion columnist Hadley Freeman in March 2009, with perhaps a pinch of satire, on the new revival. ∎

TOP: *Giorgio Armani advertising campaign for Autumn/Winter 1984, photographed by Aldo Fallai, featuring a powersuit with tailored masculine cut and wide shoulders.*

ABOVE: *Aviator Amy Johnson wears a suit in 1936 from the collection of flight clothes designed for her by Elsa Schiaparelli for her solo flight from London to Cape Town.*

'Cecil Beaton said of Garbo, "She has no friends, but a million fans are ready to die for her"'

A groomed Greta Garbo in furs, 1929.

Glitz, glamour and superstars

IDEA № 39

HOLLYWOOD AND THE TALKIES

Until the 1930s, the Paris couturiers had the last word in setting the high-fashion trends. But with the advent of the 'talkies', everything changed. Suddenly it was Hollywood costume designers who were generating new looks and trends – and communicating them to millions of viewers via the silver screen.

On 24 October 1929, Wall Street suffered its notorious crash, known as Black Thursday. It threw America into the Great Depression and sent the world economy spinning into chaos. The recession of the 1930s was a time of poverty and hardship for millions. Economic crisis meant that clothes shopping became a luxury; but women still wanted escapism.

The lives of the Hollywood stars, both on-screen and off, gave women a window into a highly desirable world of riches and glamour. Recorded sound was introduced to cinema in 1927, and cinema-goers flocked to the movies. The women dreamed of wearing Greta Garbo's hats, having Marlene Dietrich's legs, being as bottle-blond as Jean Harlow or owning Joan Crawford's *Letty Lynton* dresses. Cecil Beaton said of Garbo in *Vogue* in 1930: 'She has no friends, but a million fans are ready to die for her.'

The cinema-going public slavishly copied the on-screen trends, when they could afford it, with long bias-cut low-backed dresses in white for evening, and sharply cut wide-shouldered suits for day. Fur trims, wraps and the glitter of diamanté spread like fairy dust, adding more glamorous touches.

The Hollywood leading ladies were styled to within an inch of their lives. Presenting the perfect image was all, and cosmetic surgery was rife. The 1930s Hollywood studios spent vast sums on the wardrobes of their stars, employing costume designers such as Gilbert Adrian, Edith Head and Travis Banton to transform the girls into screen goddesses. The impact that such designers made on fashion has been as significant as any major designer working today, and they are remembered as fashion designers in their own right.

Hollywood stars continued to influence fashion with their on- and off-screen wardrobes – with Marilyn Monroe, Doris Day, Brigitte Bardot, Audrey Hepburn, Grace Kelly and Jane Fonda leading the way in the 1950s and beyond.

When, during the 1980s, designer Giorgio Armani designed costumes for the film *American Gigolo* and dressed the Hollywood stars for awards ceremonies, other designers followed suit, spotting the lucrative financial possibilities. Mutually beneficial relationships between leading designers and Hollywood stars began to blossom once more, the publicity helping both sides. And today no major fashion show is complete without its carefully dressed stars lined up in the front row for the cameras. ■

TOP: *Marlene Dietrich stars in* Angel, *1937, in a costume by Travis Banton, with fashionably wide shoulders.*

ABOVE: *Gloria Swanson poses in a long white dress, a Hollywood favourite.*

'Disposable fashion was now decidedly hip; off-the-peg clothing was more popular than couture'

An advertisement for Monsoon in 2010. High-street retailers sell mass-produced clothing at reasonable prices.

Fashion for all

MASS-MANUFACTURING

Postwar America led the boom in mass-manufacturing ready-to-wear clothes. Off-the-peg clothes that were both fashionable and affordable were to become widely available in the latter half of the twentieth century. Fashion and style would no longer be the sole preserve of the wealthy.

The United States had suffered less from the war than had Europe. In fact, between the wars it had experienced a manufacturing boom. In the clothing market America boasted the most advanced research, development, production and retailing systems. The combination during the 1920s of simple clothing silhouettes, better communication to spread the trends around the world, less expensive man-made fabrics and easy fastenings such as **the zip**, all served to benefit mass-produced clothing. The depression of the 1930s also fuelled a demand for cheaper clothes, and these could be made using the new mass-production methods in factories, using specialized sewing-machines, overlockers and power-driven cutting equipment. After 1945, Europe began to copy America's efficient production methods.

American women started to look to their domestic designers for fashion ideas, rather than merely buying copies of Parisian clothes. A new American style emerged, its emphasis on casual, interchangeable separates. These could be easily produced with the new manufacturing methods. This casual style of dress began to influence European fashion, particularly the teenage, beach- and leisurewear markets. The new clothes were sold in

high-street and department stores and, crucially, were affordable.

By the 1960s, designer fashion trends could be copied fast and efficiently. Throwaway youth fashions that had been mass-manufactured were in demand. **Disposable fashion** was now decidedly hip; off-the-peg clothing was more popular than **couture**. In order not to lose out, couture houses began to launch their own ready-to-wear lines offering mass-produced clothes in set sizes – with a designer label. 'What ready-to-wear does today ... even the Paris couturiers confirm tomorrow,' said Mary Quant. 'It has happened several times already. I think it will go on happening.' ∎

TOP: *Mass-manufacturing meant that the newly emerging phenomenon of 1950s teenagers could dress in new, smart fashions and all look the same.*

ABOVE: *This 1967 advertisement is for the polyester fibre Tergal. Mass-manufacturing and new synthetic fibres meant cheap clothes for all.*

Salvador Dali inspired this extravagant coat with eight bureau-drawer pockets by Schiaparelli, and photographed here by Cecil Beaton.

Fashion enters a dream world

IDEA № 41
SURREALISM

A jacket bearing an image of a smashed mirror. Buttons that look like beetles. A black velvet handbag in the shape of a telephone. These quirky fashion ideas were inspired by Surrealism, one of the most significant art movements to make an impact on twentieth-century fashion.

Pearl, ruby and gold brooch by Salvador Dalí, 1949. © Salvador Dalí, Fundació Gala-Salvador Dalí, DACS, 2019.

The avant-garde Surrealists shunned rational and formal thought in favour of fantasy and the creation of a dream world. In fashion, some of the most original Surrealist ideas can be seen in the 1930s work of designer Elsa Schiaparelli, whose circle of friends included the Dada and Surrealist artists Man Ray and Marcel Duchamp.

She collaborated with one of the leading lights of Surrealism, Salvador Dalí, to make a daring dress with *trompe l'oeil* rips and tears, and a hat in the shape of an upturned shoe. Controversial American socialite Wallis Simpson was bold enough to wear Schiaparelli's 1937 white silk dress printed with a vast lobster, a motif that was taken directly from a Dalí painting. With Jean Cocteau, Schiaparelli produced a coat decorated with two faces in profile, the noses nearly touching: the negative space between them formed the optical illusion of a vase of roses.

Schiaparelli found it intensely exciting to work with such original thinkers. 'Working with artists like Bébé Bérard, Jean Cocteau, Salvador Dalí, Vertès, Van Dongen, and with photographers like Hoyningen-Huene, Horst, Cecil Beaton and Man Ray, gave one a sense of exhilaration,' she wrote in her 1954 autobiography, *Shocking Life*. 'One felt supported and understood beyond the crude and boring reality of merely making a dress to sell.' In the Paris of the 1930s great Surrealist balls took place, which formed the perfect showcase for Schiaparelli's fantastical clothing.

The photographers Horst P. Horst and Man Ray both experimented with Surrealist fashion imagery for their editorial work, as well as in their advertising images and fine-art photographs. The editors of *Vogue* and *Harper's Bazaar* took note of their arresting images, and commissioned Surrealist-inspired graphics for their covers during the late 1930s.

Surrealism continues to influence fashion design, advertising and graphics. Yves Saint Laurent used Surrealist sequin lip motifs for his 1971 collection, Marc Jacobs made a dress using hand-prints at the waist in 1986, and in 1997 British department store Selfridges commissioned John Galliano and Moschino to create Surrealist window displays. For their 2009 collections, both Moschino and Viktor & Rolf incorporated pipe, cloud and bowler-hat motifs, a nod to the paintings of Surrealist artist René Magritte. A playful Surrealist legacy lives on. ■

Dress and headscarf by Elsa Schiaparelli in collaboration with Salvador Dalí, using a tear-print fabric, 1937.

Walking tall

PLATFORMS AND WEDGES

Wearing heels does not have to mean tottering along on stilettos. Platform and wedge heels give height and, sometimes, more stability, and can be hidden by long trousers or flowing skirts.

In 1937 the legendary Italian shoe designer Salvatore Ferragamo introduced a revolutionary new shoe with a wedge heel – a built-up heel that slopes down in a solid triangle to meet the sole at ground level. The design was born as much from necessity as anything else. Ferragamo had been forced to hunt around to find new materials, and owing to wartime steel shortages, he decided on cork glued together in layers. As with many fashion innovations, at first the wedge heel was scorned. But then it was copied, and subsequently became the height of fashion, with new styles developing to keep the trend alive. Designers started to cut wedge heels into sculptural shapes and added ankle straps to hold the shoes to the feet.

Shoe designer Roger Vivier is credited with inventing the modern platform shoe – with built-up heels and soles – in the mid-1930s. His first platform heel was in a chinoiserie style, and the influential fashion designer Elsa Schiaparelli showed it as part of her collection in 1939. The fashionable women of the 1940s swiftly adopted the look; heavy shoes neatly balanced the high millinery, another popular wartime trend. However, the idea was not entirely new. Vivier had been doubtless influenced by the towering chopines of sixteenth-century Venice – platform shoes soaring up to 22 centimetres (10 inches), worn by courtesans to save their dress hems from dragging in the mud.

Salvatore Ferragamo designed some of the most flamboyant and beautiful pre-war platform sandals. He embellished wooden soles with bright colours and bold patterns, and constantly experimented with new materials, from cork soles studded with brass and jewels to shoes made with snail shells, lace and **nylon**. More luxurious were his platforms covered in softly padded red suede. His 'invisible' sandal had a curved, sculptural wedge heel and an upper of nylon fishing line.

The 1970s put platforms firmly back on to the fashion stage, with wedge shoes for summer and platform boots for winter. They were the ideal footwear for the fashionable flares that kicked out at the hem. For daywear, moderate platforms and wedges were a less precarious option than traditional high heels, as they helped to elongate the figure but were easier to walk in. Platform sandals were a favourite for the evening, the delicacy of the cutaway uppers helping to soften the bulky look of the shoes with their large soles.

Vivienne Westwood revived platforms for the 1990s. Her creations included towering black patent versions punched with metal studs, and rocking-horse ballerina shoes with high curved wooden soles and ribbon straps wound around the ankles. It was time to walk tall again. ∎

ABOVE: *Carmen Miranda poses in vertiginous sandals in 1948. She was famed for her collection of platform shoes.*

BELOW: *Marilyn Monroe models wedge sandals in 1950.*

*Black patent platform shoe
with metal studs by Vivienne
Westwood.*

Supermodels, celebrities and show business

LEFT: *The runway circus – a Valentino couture show in Paris, 2006.*

ABOVE: *Elsa Schiaparelli's Circus show set a new standard, with its jugglers, clowns and ice-cream cone hats. Illustrations by Christian Bérard.*

IDEA № 43

THE FASHION SHOW AS THEATRICAL SPECTACLE

When Elsa Schiaparelli presented her 1938 Circus collection she included jugglers, tightrope walkers and clowns. The models wore outlandish hats resembling ice-cream cones and carried handbags shaped like balloons.

Live monkeys and trained dogs stalked the catwalk, helping to sell clothes printed with clowns, elephants and horses. The detail was fun and flamboyant – necklaces featuring a series of swinging trapeze artists and buttons in the shape of cavorting acrobats. Entertainment and fashion were dazzlingly combined to produce a spectacle that was more like theatre than a traditional catwalk show.

The 1930s and 1940s had seen stage sets, music and lighting added to the whole fashion show experience, but Schiaparelli was the first to theme her fashion shows, and turn them into extravagant spectacles. Her themes included musical iconography, astrology and even paganism. The press loved her for it, and she gained high-profile

clients, including Marlene Dietrich and Claudette Colbert, who were both drawn to Schiaparelli's sense of fun.

Thanks to Schiaparelli, themes, choreography, styling and music would become as central to the fashion show as the clothes. Mary Quant exemplified the mood of the 1960s by sending her models dancing down the runway. Kenzo caused a scene when he asked his models to improvise for his Jungle Jap shows in the 1970s – they frolicked, danced the can-can and even bared their breasts to the audience. But it was in the indulgent 1980s that fashion shows were at their most extravagant. With film and rock royalty in the front row, supermodels on the catwalk and the paparazzi documenting every moment and every detail, they were

epic theatrical experiences. The flamboyant Gianni Versace directed some of the most notable spectacles.

The theatrical show experience continues, with **celebrities** in attendance, the press watching every move and a flurry of social media fashion influencers ready to post the shows as they happen. Alexander McQueen asked dance choreographer Michael Clark to put together his 2004 show, so that it was more akin to performance art than fashion. McQueen also wrapped his models' heads in nets containing live butterflies, and once used a pair of robotic spray guns to colour a white dress on the catwalk. The exuberant ideas instigated by Schiaparelli continue to bring drama and magic to the fashion show. ∎

The runway for the Alexander McQueen Spring/Summer 2001 show was a mirrored cube lit from the inside, designed to represent a psychiatric ward. The finale revealed a reclining semi-naked masked woman surrounded by live moths.

'Entertainment and fashion were dazzlingly combined'

'Nylons were cheaper than silk, did not wrinkle around the ankles and added a smooth, flattering sheen to the legs'

Southend, 1938. Every fashion-conscious woman in Europe craved a pair of luxurious nylon stockings during World War II.

IDEA № 44

NYLON

The fibre nylon started with humble origins: it was first used to make toothbrush filaments in 1938. But within a decade its name had come to stand for the ultimate in fashion, every woman's wartime dream – a precious pair of nylon stockings. These became, owing to their scarcity in the wartime years, a symbol of almost unattainable luxury.

1956 magazine advertisement for Nylon by DuPont.

With a shortage of silk supplies from the Far East in the 1920s, the Americans started looking into developing possible alternatives. The chemical company DuPont established its own research division, one that was to make great strides in the world of synthetic fibres. There was a team of scientists led by Wallace Carothers created a new fibre made from immensely long chains of synthetic molecules called polymers. They patented it and named it nylon, and a legend was born.

Nylon was the first synthetic fibre, and combined extraordinary strength with elasticity. After its early use in toothbrushes, this wonder-fibre was turned to knitted hosiery in 1939, and stockings in 1940. 'Nylons', as the stockings became known, were cheaper than silk, did not wrinkle around the ankles and added a smooth, flattering sheen to the legs. Supplies were cruelly interrupted when in 1941 DuPont shifted its manufacturing of nylon to more urgent matters: parachute fabric, tents and ropes for the war effort. Women either had to wait until the war ended for their precious nylons, or buy them on the black market at exorbitant cost.

At the end of the war, Macy's department store in New York sold out of their stockings almost immediately – selling a reputed 50,000 pairs in just six hours. The press reported nylon riots on the streets of Manhattan.

In postwar years, the women's fashion industry used nylon as a substitute for silk for dresses and underwear – it felt soft and had an attractive sheen, and most importantly it was easy to launder and iron. Nylon was seen as chic and modern rather than down-market. *Harper's Bazaar* featured a fashion shoot entitled 'Nylon Tricot, Dream Fabric for Lingerie', accompanied by soft-focus shots of nylon peignoirs and gowns. Designers such as Madame Grès experimented with the fibre to make dramatic evening gowns and soft lingerie.

Today clothing in pure nylon may not be promoted as the height of high-end fashion, but nylon and the hundreds of other **synthetics** that have flooded the market have revolutionized fashion, making garments easier to wash, cheaper to buy and often more comfortable to wear. ∎

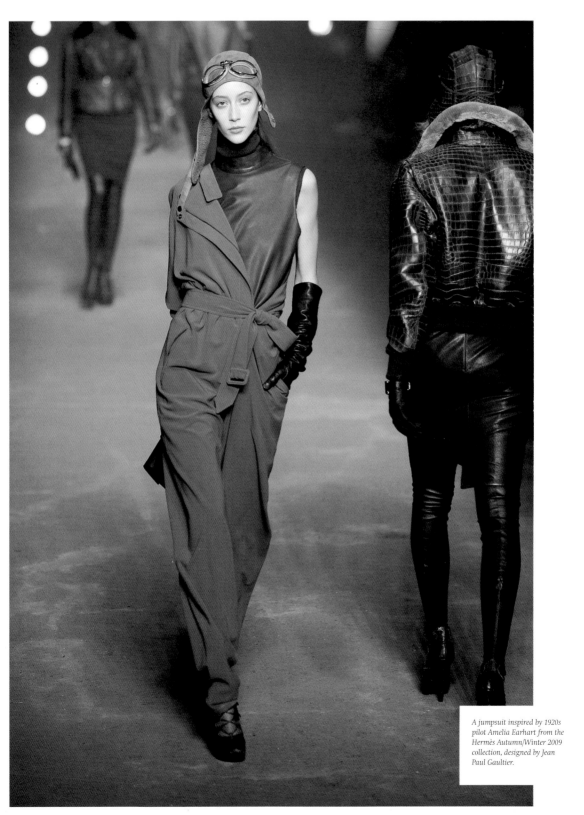

A jumpsuit inspired by 1920s pilot Amelia Earhart from the Hermès Autumn/Winter 2009 collection, designed by Jean Paul Gaultier.

The success of the all-in-one

IDEA № 45

THE JUMPSUIT

The first jumpsuits of the twentieth century were worlds away from today's alluring catwalk versions. They were worn purely for functional convenience. During World War II, American and European women donned all-in-one boiler suits in cotton or denim to work in the factories.

Elsa Schiaparelli designed stylish versions of the siren suit – jumpsuits with pockets and a large hood, perfect for impromptu moonlight trips to the bomb shelter – as famously worn by British Prime Minister Winston Churchill at the office.

By the late 1960s and early 1970s, the jumpsuit had completely crossed the line from being a practical and protective piece of clothing to being a desirable fashion item. Rather than covering up a woman's body to shield it, when executed in sexy stretch fabric a jumpsuit became slinky and provocative, perfect for some serious moves on the dancefloor. The sight of the astronauts in their NASA space suits during the much-publicized 1969 moon landings had inspired the fashion designers to rethink the all-in-one. Rudi Gernreich, Yves Saint Laurent and Donald Brooks all launched their own versions. Norma Kamali made hers in parachute **nylon**. But while the fashion industry made jumpsuits sexy enough to wear with high heels, feminists of the 1970s wore sturdier

versions of the boiler suit to make a political statement and cover their curves.

Variations on the theme include the catsuit, a skin-tight version; and the playsuit, a jumpsuit with its legs cropped into shorts. In 2008 and 2009 designers such as Alexander McQueen, Preen and Stella McCartney sent a set of flattering, narrow-legged jumpsuits sashaying down the catwalk. The all-in-one may swing in and out of fashion, but it is rarely taken up as daywear, except for manual labour. It comes into its own as night falls, as a sexier, more modern alternative to a long, fluid dress. ∎

TOP: *An American mechanic in 1943. Women working in the wartime factories wore practical all-in-one boiler suits.*

ABOVE: *Peter Brown and Pam Grier star in blaxploitation film* Foxy Brown, 1974. She sports a low-cut, figure-hugging jumpsuit.

Wartime restrictions impose a new silhouette

IDEA № 46

RATIONING

Shortages of fabric during World War II did not completely curtail fashion; rather, the restrictions forced designers and women to think creatively about their wardrobes. In Europe, the trend for wide fabric-rich skirts was put on hold, and a more frugal, streamlined silhouette with defined shoulders and knee-length skirts took centre stage.

As the war effort required essential fabric and materials, fashion designers became increasingly inventive with what remained. In Paris, the couturiers Coco Chanel and Madeleine Vionnet shut up shop, and many, including Mainbocher, Charles James and Edward Molyneux, fled abroad. Times were hard and raw materials scarce, so **couture** evening-wear hemlines became shorter, and less fabric was used for daywear. Nazi restrictions dictated that leather belts could be only 4 centimetres (1.6 inches) wide, and coats could use no more than 4 metres (157 inches) of fabric. White collars and cuffs helped to economize on the harder-to-find coloured or patterned fabric, and ribbons, unrationed as they were, proved vital for decorative detail. French women took to wearing wooden-soled shoes and were also enthusiastic recyclers of old clothes.

In Britain, the Board of Trade called on a group of designers to design stylish clothes in line with the official fabric restrictions of 1941. Hardy Amies, Edward Molyneux and Norman Hartnell were among those who rose to the challenge, and 32 designs went into mass production. They became known as Utility garments.

As the bodily silhouette grew slimmer, European hats and shoes became outsized, as if to compensate. Then when straw ran out for making straw hats, women turned to turbans, berets, veils and snoods, and began to decorate their own hats at home with scraps of fabric. And as leather became scarce, cork and wood were used for shoes with platform soles. Elsa Schiaparelli wrote in her 1954 autobiography *Shocking Life*: 'Because of the lack of buttons and safety-pins there were dog chains to close suits and to hold skirts.'

The Americans also faced rationing from 1942, and restrictions on clothing included no full evening dresses or wraps in wool, and no bias-cut sleeves or wide leather belts. The American designers, such as Claire McCardell, were innovative, creating, for example, the 'capsule wardrobe' of coordinates, so that the same tops and bottoms could be mixed and matched in different combinations to suit the varying sartorial demands of each occasion. ■

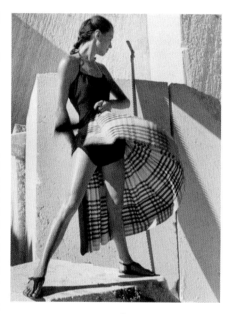

Innovative US designer Claire McCardell designed this modern wrap skirt and bathing suit as early as 1946.

A British punk in 2003 with customized trousers and leather jacket.

Knitting for victory

FAR LEFT: *A Max Factor representative paints stockings onto a woman's leg in 1940.*

LEFT: *A stylish wedding guest wears a knitted hat in 1940, at the start of World War II.*

IDEA № 47
MAKE DO AND MEND

When World War II broke out in 1939, women had little idea of the impact it would have – not only in terms of fatalities, but also the way in which everyday life would be transformed. Wartime restrictions forced designers and ordinary women to be resourceful when it came to fashion, and this led to new ideas, materials and trends.

Domestic **rationing** and the German occupation of Europe both took their toll on fashion. Voluminous designs and needless embellishments were out of the question. Silk was used for making parachutes and not for elegant ladies' dresses. The British government advised: 'When you feel tired of your old clothes, remember that by making them do, you are contributing to some part of an aeroplane, a gun or a tank.'

The era of Make Do and Mend was therefore a time of enforced creativity. Women started knitting and recycling old clothes – sewing ribbons onto old dresses, and using domestic furnishing fabrics to make coats and other clothing. It was not unknown for dressing gowns to be fashioned from

captured German flags. The Italian shoe designer Salvatore Ferragamo used cork, Bakelite and raffia to make wedge heels. Vaseline, cocoa powder and charcoal made for alternative cosmetics, and women pencilled seams up the back of their legs with liquid gravy browning to create the illusion of stockings. Rather than wearing conventional matching suits, the astute mixed separates to suggest the impression of a larger wardrobe.

The end of the war did not mark the end of such creativity. The **hippies** in the late 1960s and early 1970s also embraced the idea of craft and homespun clothing, embellishing their **jeans** and jackets with patches and beads. Similarly, **punks** customized

leather jackets with chains, made jewellery from safety pins and creatively ripped their T-shirts.

During the 1990s recycling became fashionable. Expensive vintage boutiques sprang up alongside traditional charity shops, and thrift was no longer viewed with disdain. Designer Helen Storey launched a collection called Second Life, consisting of altered and customized vintage clothes. By the turn of the century, craft, homespun and handmade clothes had become hip again, and young craft-inspired designers could now sell directly to the consumer on **the Internet**, bypassing traditional retail outlets such as shops. The Make Do and Mend aesthetic was still alive and kicking. ∎

Punks and policemen walk on air

LEFT: *1980s British skinheads wear DM boots as part of their street-style uniform.*

ABOVE: *The men who invented the DM boot, Dr Klaus Maertens (left) and Herbert Funck, photographed in the 1960s.*

IDEA Nº 48

DR. MARTENS BOOTS

Walking on air is not just the stuff of dreams. When a 25-year-old doctor in the German Army, Dr Klaus Maertens, thought up the air-cushioned sole after breaking his foot skiing in the Bavarian Alps during World War II, he can have had no idea that his boot would go on to become the favourite footwear of skinheads, **punk**s and football fans.

At the end of the war, Maertens joined forces with a mechanical engineer, Herbert Funck, to go into business manufacturing the new boots. At first they used scavenged materials. The rubber for the soles was bought from former Luftwaffe airfields, metal regimental numbers from old army jackets were reused as eyelets, and the leather was garnered from army officers' trousers.

The new air-cushioned boots first sold for their comfort and sturdiness, with factory and construction workers soon recognizing their practical advantages. In 1960 Maertens sold the UK patent rights to the British firm Griggs, which began making the boots in England in 1960 in black and cherry-red versions, adding the distinctive yellow outer stitching. The unique air-cushioned soles were trademarked under the name AirWair.

British skinheads adopted the boots in the 1960s, wearing them with skinny trousers; in the 1970s punks customized them with paint and chains, while football fans adorned them with their team colours. Even as the boots' popularity spread through the sub-cultures, Dr. Martens also became part of the official British police uniform in the 1970s.

But it took two **Japanese design**ers to help the boots find a place in mainstream fashion. Yohji Yamamoto and Rei Kawakubo of Comme des Garçons put them on the catwalk. Ideally coupled with 501 **jeans**, and black leather or bomber jackets, DMs,

as they had become commonly known, were part of the unisex urban uniform of the 1980s.

Nike introduced air-cushioned soles for running shoes in 1979, releasing the iconic Air Max trainer in 1987, while DMs remained favourites with students, goths, **grunge** fans and indie kids. And so the new technology stemming from Dr Klaus Maertens' accident in the mountains continues to be felt under the feet of millions. ∎

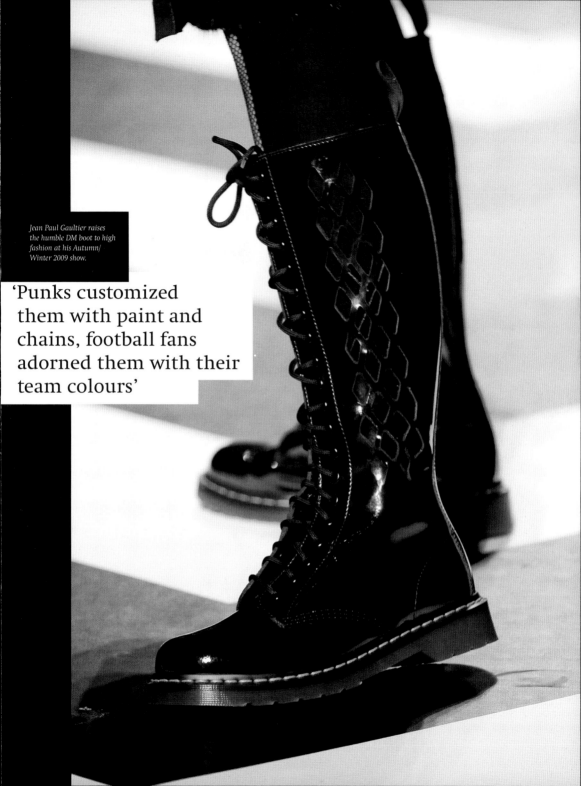

Jean Paul Gaultier raises the humble DM boot to high fashion at his Autumn/Winter 2009 show.

'Punks customized them with paint and chains, football fans adorned them with their team colours'

'Paris is now just one fashion player'

Fashion's favourite city loses her crown

IDEA № 49

PARIS CHALLENGED

In the first half of the twentieth century, Paris was still the undisputed queen of fashion, its haute **couture** collections setting the international trends. Fifty years later, at the turn of the new millennium, New York, London and Milan had all become serious contenders for the crown.

Over the next ten years Sydney, Mumbai and Tokyo all began to host major fashion events, and by the early 2000s even more cities opened their arms to the international markets.

After World War II, the United States was a world leader in manufacturing, and was offering cheaper and better-quality fashion. For sartorial ideas, affluent Americans in the 1950s looked to their home-grown designers, including Mainbocher and Norman Norell, rather than solely to Paris. America became known for its **sport**y leisurewear, and New York Fashion Week started in 1943, under the title Press Week, because the war made it impossible to travel to the Paris shows. It became a crucial fixture on the international fashion circuit.

Milan Fashion Week also became a regular feature on the calendar of buyers and the fashion press, evolving after the war, when new Italian designers such as Simonetta and Alberto Fabiani began to make waves with their brightly patterned clothes. A group of ten designers from Rome and Milan put on a show in Florence in 1951 called the Alta Moda Pronta, which grew into a biannual event at the Pitti Palace. It put designers such as Emilio Pucci and Roberto Capucci on the international fashion map. From the late 1970s, Milan rather than Florence hosted the Italian ready-to-wear shows.

During the 1960s the fashion industry turned its gaze on London, whose youthful and often irreverent trends were exerting a big influence on international fashion. The British Fashion Council formed in 1983 and raised the profile of the London fashion shows with its organization of London Fashion Week for press and buyers.

Paris unquestionably remains the centre of haute couture and still stages highly influential shows of ready-to-wear womenswear twice a year. But the French capital cannot afford to rest on its laurels and rely on past reputation alone – the buyers and press who flock there are well aware of what other global cities have to offer. And with live streaming, shows can be watched on computers around the world as they happen. Paris is now just one player among many on a busy international fashion stage. ∎

Fashion press and buyers flock to the biannual Milan ready-to-wear shows.

Models make the A-list

IDEA Nº 50

THE SUPERMODEL

Jean Shrimpton, Twiggy, Lauren Hutton, Jerry Hall and Kate Moss are some of the beauties who have acquired supermodel status. When the girls became household names outside the fashion industry, the public began to view them as fashion icons and personalities. Often they outshone the clothes on their backs.

TOP: *Lisa Fonssagrives, arguably the first supermodel, poses for photographer Horst P. Horst in 1949.*

ABOVE: *Kate Moss as a young supermodel, 1997.*

Originally, models were pretty girls used to show clothes, and not generally known or promoted by name. The Swedish model Lisa Fonssagrives, who rose to fame in the 1940s, changed all this. She is acclaimed by some as the first supermodel, not least for appearing on more than 200 covers of *Vogue*. A modest girl (for the highest-paid model of her era) she told *Time* magazine: 'It is always the dress, it is never, never the girl. I'm just a good clothes hanger.' Others regard 1960s model Lesley Hornby – better known as Twiggy on account of her diminutive stature – as the first supermodel.

During the 1970s, the American models were the big stars, and their modelling careers often led them into acting roles. Lauren Hutton negotiated a vast contract with the cosmetics company Revlon – the most lucrative secured by a model at the time – paving the way for future contracts in the industry. In the 1980s, with the increase of fashion and fragrance advertising on television and large billboards, the public simply could not miss the airbrushed faces of the supermodels. And astute models such as Christie Brinkley realized that endorsing products not only brought higher fees, but also raised their public profile and celebrity status – which could only lead to more work.

However, the true decade of the supermodel was the 1990s. Linda Evangelista, Naomi Campbell, Christy Turlington, Cindy Crawford, Claudia Schiffer and Kate Moss, among others, became household names. They commanded vast fees, signed contracts with cosmetics giants, frequented chat shows and were routinely mentioned in gossip columns – just like the movie stars. Nor did the passage of years dent their earnings potential. Elle Macpherson launched a successful underwear company and Christy Turlington brought out a clothing collection. Kate Moss followed in 2007 with a collection for Topshop. Linda Evangelista was not quite as un-assuming as Fonssagrives before her, famously declaring in 1990: 'We have this expression, Christy and I: We don't wake up for less than $10,000 a day.'

Now, however, the true age of the supermodel has passed. Actresses are likely to be used for brand endorsement, especially for cosmetics companies, and few models today are household names. ■

'They commanded vast fees and were routinely mentioned in gossip columns – just like the movie stars'

Photographer Peter Lindbergh enjoys the attentions of some of the leading 1990s supermodels: Christy Turlington, Tatjana Patitz, Naomi Campbell, Cindy Crawford and Linda Evangelista.

Sex-bomb Ursula Andress wears her famous white bikini in the Bond film Dr. No in 1962.

More powerful than
an atomic explosion

THE BIKINI

*Louis Réard's risqué bikini of 1946
caused a sensation. Unable to find
a respectable model to wear his
new creation, the job went to this
stripper from the Casino de Paris.*

The bikini has been likened to 'a picture frame that highlights all the erogenous zones', and there is no doubting its erotic appeal. When it was first shown at a 1946 fashion event in Paris, its inventor, Louis Réard, found that no model would agree to wear it.

In fact, two men are accredited with the invention of the bikini in 1946, independently of each other – Réard, and Jacques Heim. Heim first called the garment the Atome, but Réard named it the bikini after the Pacific atoll on which the Americans performed a nuclear test in July 1946, and this was the name that caught on. Réard hired a stripper called Micheline Bernardini to show off this novel creation, so daringly revealing for the times – just a bra top worn with two lower triangles of fabric held together by strings.

Within a decade, French girls were parading their summer tans in bikinis trimmed with pretty artificial flowers or animal motifs. The Americans were less adventurous, and did not fully accept the bikini until as late as the mid-1960s. Similarly, in other European countries the bikini was slow to be accepted and in Italy, Spain and Portugal it was even banned.

The bikini was the perfect vehicle for up-and-coming starlets to advertise their pert figures. It could only help their careers. Rita Hayworth was famously photographed for the cover of *Life* magazine in a white bikini. Jayne Mansfield attended a ball in 1956 wearing nothing but a leopard-print bikini. The images of Raquel Welch in her animal-skin bikini in *One Million*

Years B.C. (1966) and of Bond girl Ursula Andress in *Dr. No* (1962), emerging from the surf, have become icons of the age.

Réard had advertised his creation as 'smaller than the smallest swimsuit', but it was to get smaller still. Those who had thought Réard's early version risqué would have been outraged by the string bikini of the 1970s – it comprised four minuscule triangles of fabric fastened with strings around the body. It was almost nonexistent, and allowed for a nearly seamless tan.

Public attitudes to nudity were changing fast. Today the bikini is accepted on every beach in the West, and is worn by women of all generations, from small children to grandmothers. ■

Decadent dresses in an impoverished world

IDEA № 52
THE NEW LOOK

Scandal was in the air when Christian Dior launched his 1947 **couture** collection. He called it the Corolle line because his voluptuous skirts exploded outwards from the tiniest of waists like a corolla of flower petals, but it was quickly dubbed the New Look by *Harper's Bazaar* editor Carmel Snow, and this was the name that stuck.

Dior used many metres of fabric for these huge dresses. As there were still severe shortages of materials all over Europe, the designer seemed to be mocking the **rationing** of World War II, deliberately flaunting the strict rules of **Make Do and Mend**.

Women were both mesmerized and horrified by the extravagance of the collection, and indeed it represented a startling contrast to the workaday overalls and utility clothing of wartime Europe. These new designs suggested abundance and a time of plenty. Under the dresses, waists had to be nipped in with waspie corsets, and hip pads made a woman's figure under her skirts look even more voluptuous. *Vogue* reported: 'Dior is the new name in Paris. With his first collection he not only shot to fame, but retrieved the general situation by reviving interest in a somewhat uninspiring season.'

By referring back to the hourglass silhouette of the nineteenth century, a time when middle- and upper-class women led highly pampered lives, Dior and his dresses offered women a dream of optimism and affluence after the dark years of the war. It is fair to point out that the trend had been inching this way even before the outbreak of war in 1939, with the designers Cristobal Balenciaga, Jacques Fath and Pierre Balmain all beginning to introduce wider skirts – but Dior's timing was impeccable with his post-war launch.

Scandalized by the extravagance – as much as 15 metres (49 feet) of fabric could go into a day dress and 25 metres (82 feet) into an evening dress – angry mobs picketed the house of Dior. A model in Paris was stripped of her dress in public, and politicians fulminated against the needless waste of fabric. But the controversy only lent further publicity to the trend, and as postwar shortages gradually came to an end, opposition soon ceased. And women loved what they saw. The New Look remained firmly established as the dominant fashionable silhouette until the mid-1950s. ∎

Christian Dior's Bar Suit, from his revolutionary 1947 couture collection, was a tempting proposal for women who had suffered fabric restrictions and rationing during World War II.

This dress by Christian Dior from c. 1949 epitomizes the voluptuous New Look silhouette and decadent use of fabric.

Drip-dry and wrinkle-free

IDEA № 53
SYNTHETICS

From **nylon** to polyester, the gradual development of synthetics over the course of the twentieth century has changed the way we dress today. Synthetics have several advantages over natural fibres, among them allowing clothes to dry faster, to wear better, to stretch more and to wrinkle less.

A model wears a dress made from Dracon polyester fibre and cotton in 1969.

Nylon was introduced in 1938 by DuPont, becoming the first truly synthetic fibre on the market for domestic use. It initially allowed women during and after World War II to wear stockings that did not run or wrinkle, and was later used for underwear and womenswear. Nylon combined strength and elasticity.

Since then synthetic fibres have become an essential component in clothing manufacture and design; prominent fibres include acrylic, nylon, polyester and Spandex (also known as **Lycra** and elastane). Designer Elsa Schiaparelli was excited by the new fibres and worked with textile manufacturers, using fabrics such as cellophane for her **couture** garments.

Drip-dry fabric was to save millions of housewives from the drudgery of drying and ironing and coincided usefully with the demise of domestic service and the advent of domestic appliances such as washing machines. Cotton–acrylic mixes of the 1950s made up some of the very first drip-dry fabric, and the polyester fibre that followed was snapped up by clothing firms and used to make even more efficient drip-dry clothing. Synthetics also ensured that colours did not run in the wash.

By the 1960s a host of new synthetics had flooded the market and were driving fashion trends. Dynel and Teklan were used to make fake furs and fake hair for wigs. Designers experimented with plastic and heat-fusing techniques – the hip cats of Swinging London wore wipe-clean clothing in PVC and vinyl. Dacron, a type of polyester, was used in arrestingly bright colours. Textile companies worked with designers such as Mary Quant to raise the profile of the new fabrics and fibres.

Synthetics continued to be associated with disposable and cheaper lines, but by the end of the millennium it had become acceptable, and even expected, that synthetics would be added to natural fibres. This combination retained the natural look of a fabric such as silk or cotton but added strength, stretch or anti-wrinkle qualities. The introduction of micro-fibres revolutionized **sport**swear and underwear, with lightweight second-skin fabrics that were tough and strong.

The benefits of synthetics have been widespread, particularly for sportswear, underwear and accessories. The extra stretch and durability, together with the easy-care qualities and cost-effectiveness, have undoubtedly revolutionized fashion. ∎

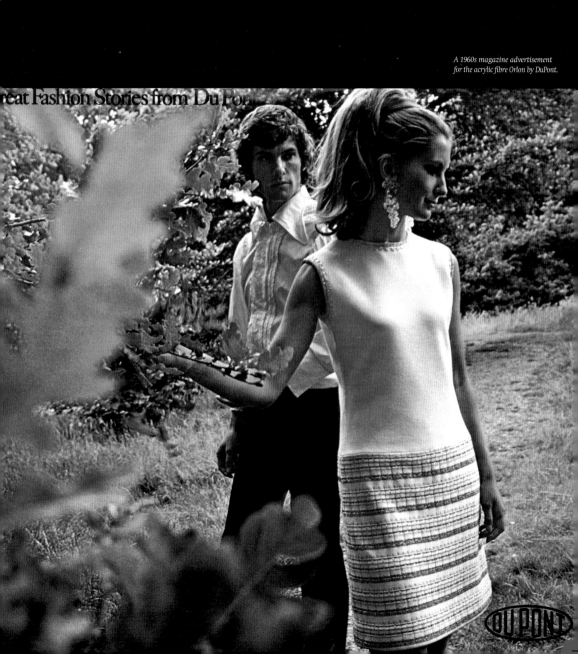

'The hip cats of Swinging London wore wipe-clean clothing in PVC and vinyl'

A 1960s magazine advertisement for the acrylic fibre Orlon by DuPont.

Great Fashion Stories from Du Pont

DUPONT

The power of youth

TEENAGE FASHION

1950s teenagers hang out at The Two I's Coffee Bar in London's Soho.

There has never been a world without teenagers – yet only relatively recently have they been considered on their own terms, and not as slightly older children or slightly younger adults. Between the wars young people began to have their own fashions and trends, but it was in the 1950s that teenagers gained power and prominence as a distinct group.

The postwar period was one of prosperity for Britain and, particularly, the United States. Affluence brought a new freedom to ordinary families, and teenagers were not exempt. They had both spending power and leisure time – a heady combination that advertisers were quick to target. They became a distinct group with their own looks, attitudes and styles. Teenagers were eager to spend their cash on clothes, records and desirable consumer goods. In rock and roll – Satan's music, as their parents called it – they had their own defining music. They hung out in soda shops (in America) and milk bars (in Britain), they rode scooters or drove convertibles, they went to hops, proms and dances, and they dressed in a completely different way from their parents.

American styles via television, cinema and music were influential on European teenagers. James Dean was the ultimate teen rebel, along with Paul Newman and Marlon Brando; Marilyn Monroe, Doris Day and Elizabeth Taylor were models for the girls; and Elvis Presley, Bill Haley and Jerry Lee Lewis provided the rock-and-roll soundtrack.

Girls no longer wanted to dress exactly like their mothers, in neat suits. They wanted looser, less formal clothes that emphasized their youth and independence. They wore circle skirts with wide belts, topped with white shirts, sweaters or cardigans; or floral-print dresses with full skirts and a scarf tied at the neck. Polo necks, **jeans** and pedal-pushers offered a more casual look. Hollywood movie stars inspired the teen sweater-girl style, in which provocatively tight jumpers were stretched over thrusting breasts.

By the 1960s, the teen and youth market was leading mainstream fashion. The young wanted disposable clothes that they could change regularly as trends ebbed and flowed; and the record companies, fashion labels and shops increasingly began to employ, or be run by, young people themselves. Within a decade, the generation gap had widened dramatically.

Teenagers were now a sociological group of their own, with an influence and spending power that would only increase as the decades wore on. ∎

Tokyo 16-year-olds create their own carefully styled street look wearing labels including Fila, Converse and Chanel, 2006.

'An emblem of toughness'

A leather jacket by John Richmond for Spring/Summer 2006.

For punks, rockers and rebels

IDEA № 55
THE BLACK LEATHER JACKET

The anti-establishment sartorial statement of **punk**s and bikers, the black leather jacket used to signify rebellion. Today it is a classic fashion staple, almost as common as **jeans** or **trainers**. Yet, although its associations with dissatisfied youth may have been diluted, the black leather jacket is unlikely ever to lose its aura of cool.

As with many pieces of clothing popularized as street fashion, the origins of the black leather jacket lie with the military. They were issued to German pilots in World War I, while German submarine crews, bomber pilots and members of the SS wore them in World War II. A seductive Marlene Dietrich immortalized the look for women in the film *Dishonored* (1931), starring as a Viennese prostitute turned secret agent – clad in black leather.

After the wars, the black leather jacket became the uniform of American policemen, selected for its resilience. As an emblem of toughness as well as for its protective qualities, it was taken up in the 1950s by bikers – often dissatisfied ex-servicemen – who congregated in gangs or at motorbike rallies and gained a reputation for violence and hard drinking. Their black leather Perfecto or Bronx jackets, worn with jeans and white scarves, looked tough and proudly working class, in an era where respectable men wore suits. The few girls who dared to join the biker boys went for unisex leathers too. László Benedek's film *The Wild One* (1953) chronicled this hedonistic yet intimidating group, casting the brooding Marlon Brando as the black-leather-clad lead.

Though Yves Saint Laurent dared to put a black leather jacket on the catwalk in 1960, it was Britain's rockers who at that time made the black

leather jacket their own. Greasers, punks and heavy-metal fans all wore versions of the black leather jacket, while in the United States it was taken up by members of the Black Power movement, the Black Panthers. Gay men wore leather clothing, including leather jackets, as a symbol of their sexual status – they were sometimes referred to as leathermen. Both Chanel and Versace later put the leather jacket on the catwalk and soon enough it became part of the respectable unisex street uniform of the 1980s, especially when combined with Levi's jeans and **Dr. Martens boots**.

And the leather jacket, post 1960s, was not restricted to the original Perfecto biker style. A leather jacket could be tailored or bomber-style, long and sleek or short and cropped. Designers reinterpreted both classic and new shapes in leather, and did not restrict the colour to black. Textured skins such as suede, or leather with an ostrich or alligator finish, added a new exotic interest to classic styles. Leather was no longer a symbol of rebellion. ∎

TOP: *Marlon Brando in cult biker movie* The Wild One *in 1953.*

ABOVE: *Marlene Dietrich stars as a prostitute turned secret agent in* Dishonored, *1931.*

From underwear to outerwear

THE T-SHIRT

When Marlon Brando dramatically appeared on cinema screens in *A Streetcar Named Desire*, his clothing came as a profound shock to most viewers. His character – the sensual, violent Stanley Kowalski – wore a ripped, sweat-soaked T-shirt. This was 1951, and T-shirts at this time were known only as men's underwear.

But what Brando wore to such shocking effect in 1951 was – ironically – to become one of the most popular garments of the latter half of the twentieth century. T-shirts were worn as undershirts by the American military, and during World War II troops had begun to strip down to their T-shirts in order to keep cool while working. But such a thing was never done in a civilian environment. It took Brando's iconic screen presence – along with that of James Dean in *Rebel Without a Cause* (1955) – to sell this novel idea to 1950s youth. They enthusiastically took to white T-shirts, and wore them as symbols of rebellion and individuality.

In the 1960s women took up the T-shirt. Tie-dyed and screen-printed motifs added pattern and colour, and teamed with long hair, **jeans** and a string of beads, the T-shirt became a unisex uniform of the 1970s. T-shirts provided a classic means for promoting bands, activists, politicians and almost anyone else with a message, and it was not long before advertisers, too, discovered their lucrative power.

Katharine Hamnett was more thoughtful than most with her use of slogan T-shirts for her Choose Life collection in 1984. Hamnett devotees wore T-shirts emblazoned with bold messages in capital letters: Ban Pollution, Heroin Free Zone, Worldwide Nuclear Ban Now. Her garments gave their wearers the chance to make potent political statements without opening their mouths.

Hamnett herself was amazed by the initial reaction to her slogan T-shirts. 'Hard to believe it now, but they used to be considered offensive,' she said. 'In the early 1980s American *Vogue* finally deigned to visit my showroom, which was at the time a very chic faux cave, and when they saw T-shirts saying "Love" and "Peace" they spun, literally spun, on their kitten heels and walked straight out.' ∎

ABOVE: *Marlon Brando shocks audiences in cult movie* A Streetcar Named Desire *(1951).*

RIGHT: *Johnny Rotten of the Sex Pistols poses in a confrontational punk T-shirt.*

'They were worn as symbols of rebellion and individuality'

Save the Sea T-shirt by Katharine Hamnett for YOOXYGEN, 2010.

A pair of killer heels

THE STILETTO

In Italian, a stiletto is a type of small dagger. The shoe that bears its name was launched in Italy in the early 1950s, and changed the female fashion silhouette irrevocably, as well as the way a woman walked and moved in her clothes. A fetish object as much as a fashion item, the stiletto heel has an eternal, defiantly sexual, allure.

Senso boot for Autumn/Winter 1998. Design and drawing by Manolo Blahnik.

It is still not entirely clear who first came up with the idea. Shoe designers Salvatore Ferragamo and Roger Vivier both lay claim to the invention of the thin steel reinforcing bar that provides the core support to a stiletto heel. High heels were not a new phenomenon, but before the 1950s they had to be thick and sturdy if they were to be very tall, their cores being made of a relatively weak material such as wood.

When Christian Dior added shoes to his stable in 1953, he asked Roger Vivier to be his designer. Vivier introduced the stiletto heel to the Dior clients the following year, while in Italy Salvatore Ferragamo designed his own version. Whoever was first, this was clearly an idea whose moment had come. Now women could weave high above the pavements with confidence, on just a skinny support. The movie stars and pin-up girls loved them, including Jayne Mansfield, Bettie Page and Marilyn Monroe.

The high stiletto goes in and out of fashion, but many women (and the men who watch them) have a never-ending love affair with these often-punishing inventions. They straighten the ankle, arch the foot into a point, tilt the pelvis, lift the buttocks and raise the bust, tilting the posture into a sexy stance. Stiletto heels force a woman to slow down and encourage her hips to swing as she walks. They flatter the figure by elongating and slimming the leg, making a woman taller, and finishing everything off with a pretty pointed foot. No wonder so many women put up with the undeniable discomfort: they feel transformed into *femmes fatales* when they put on their shoes.

Both the French designer Christian Louboutin and the London-based Spanish designer Manolo Blahnik continue to dress their clients in gravity-defying stilettos, as do Jimmy Choo, Rupert Sanderson and Givenchy. But the Italian houses still lead the way, with Prada, Miu Miu, Gucci and Dolce & Gabbana keeping hold of the stiletto crown. ∎

'Stiletto heels force a woman to slow down and encourage her hips to swing as she walks'

An image from the famous shoot for Charles Jourdan's Autumn 1979 campaign by legendary photographer Guy Bourdin.

The denim revolution

LEVI STRAUSS OVERALLS

IDEA № 58

JEANS

Whether they be bootleg, skinny, baggy or low-slung, denim jeans are a unisex mainstay of Western fashion for both young and old. Almost everyone owns a pair of jeans. The trousers that started as masculine workwear can today be respectably smartened up with heels and a jacket and regarded as feminine and chic.

They are not quite yet acceptable in financial, trading or legal offices where a suit is *de rigueur*, but they have certainly come a long way from their humble beginnings.

Hardwearing denim trousers were worn in nineteenth-century Europe, but jeans as we know them today were launched in 1873 by Jacob Davis and Levi Strauss in the small gold rush town of San Francisco. They wanted a robust product for the tough outdoor world of the Far West, and their breakthrough was to use robust copper rivets to strengthen the pockets and points of strain. A numbering system helped retailers to identify the different styles of the so-called 'waist overalls', and the best quality were given the number 501. Blue denim jeans soon became the workwear of cowboys, lumberjacks, farmers and ranchers.

American teenage rebels in the 1950s started to wear jeans, encouraged by the silver-screen appearances of denim-clad idols, such as Marilyn Monroe in *Clash by Night* (1952) and James Dean in *Rebel Without a Cause* (1955). Jeans were imported to Europe, and Lee, Wrangler and Levi's gave the teenagers on both sides of the pond a taste of postwar prosperity and youthful identity.

By the 1970s blue jeans were the uniform of youth. Girls and boys wore matching flared versions, along with their long hair and beads. This was also the era of the first branded designer jeans, with Fiorucci, Ralph Lauren, Gloria Vanderbilt and Calvin Klein all cashing in. Bianca Jagger and Jacqueline Kennedy Onassis became fans of the new designer denim. Klein controversially hired the teenage Brooke Shields for a series of provocative jeans ads, shot and directed by Richard Avedon. In one dynamic stills photograph she looks like she is about to whip off her shirt. In another commercial she coos: 'You wanna know what comes between me and my Calvins? Nothing.' *The Sunday Times* reported that sales of blue jeans turned Klein's company from a $25 million into a $180-million business in just a year.

Levi's 501s themselves swung back into fashion for men and women during the 1980s, with a stream of cult TV and cinema ads, the most notorious featuring the model Nick Kamen

TOP: *High-waisted jeans on a Los Angeles street in 1979.*

ABOVE: *1950s magazine advertisement for Levi's. This was the decade that jeans, used as working men's overalls, become fashionable unisex casualwear for teenagers.*

OPPOSITE PAGE: *The controversial Calvin Klein Jeans advertisement photographed by Richard Avedon, featuring a teenage Brooke Shields, 1980.*

stripping to his boxer shorts in a launderette. During the following decade the bootleg jean and low-slung hipster trousers were the dominant trends in denim. New brands started to appear on the market, such as Earl Jean, 7 for All Mankind and True Religion Brand Jeans. Some, catering specifically for women, focused on flattering cuts and added stretch – and bore a high price tag to match. Jeans had made the dramatic leap from men's workwear to women's designer wear in just 100 years. ∎

French university students dance the jitterbug in sneakers, Paris, 1949.

The street's favourite footwear

Run-DMC helped to make Adidas trainers hip, with their single 'My Adidas' of 1986.

IDEA Nº 59

TRAINERS

Once used only for **sport**, today's modern trainers are a world away from their athletic origins. They are as ubiquitous as a pair of **jeans** or a white T-shirt, and are worn every day as part of a casual dressed-down uniform.

Their forerunners, rubber-soled canvas plimsolls, had been worn on the beach and for sport since the late 1800s. Keds, one of the early successful plimsoll brands, was introduced to the United States in 1916. The shoes became known as sneakers owing to their quiet rubber soles, which allowed the wearer to sneak around noiselessly. Next came the popular Converse All Star shoe in 1917. Converse was canny enough to see, early on, the business benefits of celebrity endorsement, persuading basketball legend Chuck Taylor to add his signature to the All Star motif in the 1920s, and badminton star Jack Purcell to endorse the Converse Jack Purcell sneaker in the 1930s.

American teenagers started to wear trainers or sneakers as casualwear off the sportsfield during the 1950s, inspired by movie stars such as James Dean seen in his Levi's and white sneakers in *Rebel Without a Cause*.

Meanwhile in Germany, the two Dassler brothers were developing running shoes with leather uppers. In 1948, the brothers argued, split and never spoke to each other again, but each went on to form a brand that would be a market leader in sports clothes and trainers – Puma and Adidas. Nike, named after the ancient Greek winged goddess of victory, launched in 1971 in Oregon.

The crossover from sport to fashion continued after athlete Tommie Smith wore Puma Suede trainers (known as Clydes) to win the 200 metres at the Mexican Olympics in 1968. He raised his fist in the Black Power salute when he received his gold medal and the shoes became a cult item on the street, associated with Black Pride. Soon football fans started to wear trainers, and a surge in the popularity of jogging took sports shoes onto the street. By the 1980s trainers had become universally popular, and the sports brands put aside large marketing budgets for advertising and celebrity endorsement.

By the turn of the millennium, high-fashion designers were teaming up with leading trainer brands to get their cut of the lucrative market. Yohji Yamamoto's collaboration with Adidas brought the consumer sleek black-and-white three-stripe trainers for the cult Y-3 range. Stella McCartney took a more practical approach with Adidas for a range that aimed to make outdoor sports hip, with tennis and running shoes. Paul Smith designed a limited-edition Reebok running shoe in a series of bright colour combinations, while Mihara Yasuhiro's trainers for Puma focused on quirky fun with studs, fur, stripes and metallics. These are certainly shoes for the street – their impact would be wasted on the gym. ∎

MAIN PIC: *The oldest known Converse All Star basketball shoe in existence, c. 1918.*

TOP LEFT: *Lunar trainer by Nike, created for the Beijing Olympics in 2008.*

BOTTOM LEFT: *Trainer by Adidas for Spring/Summer 2010.*

TOP RIGHT: *Gola Go Future White high top. With a fondness for punchy block colour and cartoon capers, Jean-Charles de Castelbajac has injected his creative genius and love for quirky Pop-art styling into an exclusive collection for British sportswear brand Gola for Autumn/Winter 2010.*

BOTTOM RIGHT: *Archive 1980s-style Suede trainer by Puma.*

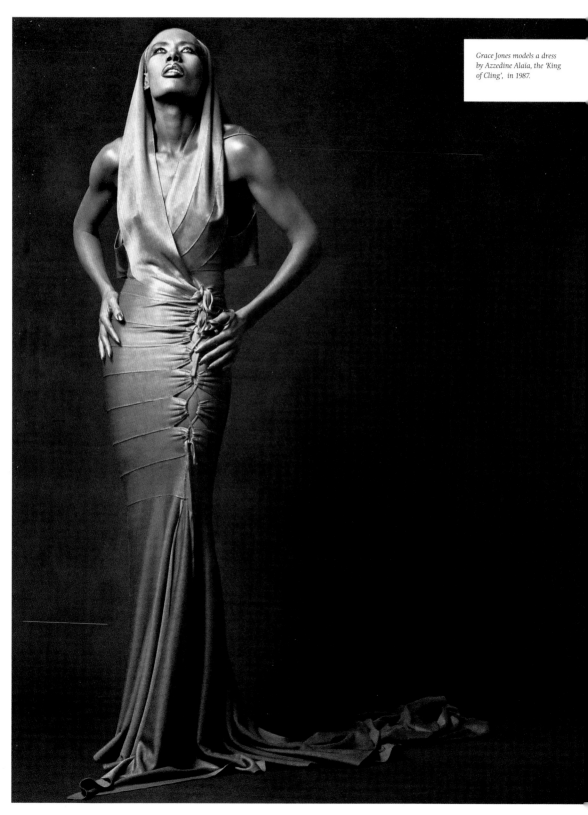

Grace Jones models a dress by Azzedine Alaïa, the 'King of Cling', in 1987.

The next wonder-fibre

IDEA № 60

LYCRA

Not long after they invented **nylon**, the scientists at the chemical company DuPont gave us a new wonder-fibre: Lycra. This super-stretchy invention was a complete revolution; no previous textile had ever behaved like it.

Garments incorporating Lycra fibres would stretch and bounce without losing their shape, and dry out quickly. They could be dyed and machine-washed, and unlike rubber, contact with perspiration and cosmetics would not cause them to deteriorate.

DuPont invented Lycra, also known as Spandex or elastane, in the late 1950s as a replacement for rubber in corsetry. By the 1960s Lycra had become a crucial component of swimsuits, ski-suits and the new virtually seamless underwear. Tight shiny clothes were essential for any girl who wanted to rock it on the dancefloor or in the aerobics studio in the 1970s. Lycra-mix leggings, leotards and second-skin **jeans** clung glossily and satisfyingly to the body without sagging.

Leading fashion designers noted the benefits that Lycra had brought to hosiery and underwear in the 1980s, and became interested in experimenting with stretch fabrics. The Tunisian designer Azzedine Alaïa became known as the 'King of Cling' because of his fondness for body-hugging stretch dresses. He produced skin-tight outfits of Lycra and wool, which he moulded to the body with the help of strategically placed zips. 'Magazine editors and **the supermodel**s – Christy, Cindy, Naomi and Linda – knew better than anyone what an Alaïa

dress could do for them: it has the pleasing effect of plastic surgery without the mess,' said fashion editor Susannah Frankel in 2003.

Hervé Léger designed his first signature bandage dresses in 1989. He used rainbow-coloured horizontal bands of wool or silk, often mixed with Lycra, to create frocks that encircled and contained the curves not unlike early twentieth-century control underwear. In the late 2000s Canadian designer Mark Fast introduced his sexy skin-revealing dresses, in a similar vein to Alaïa's and described by *Vogue* as 'gossamer thin but strong as a pair of Spanx' (control underwear). Clothes never needed to sag again – and nor did the flesh inside. ∎

TOP: *Lycra gives swimwear and underwear the stretch it needs to mould tightly to the body.*

ABOVE: *A signature bandage dress by Hervé Léger, 1997, emphasizing the curves while moulding the figure.*

Rock royalty makes fashion headlines

IDEA № 61
POP STARS

The first major pop stars were the crooners of the 1930s and 1940s such as Bing Crosby and Frank Sinatra, and then came the 1950s, rock and roll and Elvis Presley. But it was the Beatles that set the pop standard for the stars who would follow in their wake.

The Fab Four were pop and rock royalty, writing their own material, hugely influencing fashion, lifestyle and music in the UK and beyond, and providing teenagers and twenty-somethings with style icons to aspire to.

Teddy boys adopted the rock-and-roll elements of Elvis's dress in the 1950s, while in the following decade men emulated the Beatles' haircuts, skinny suits and Nehru collars. By the 1960s women had also started overtly to emulate their pop and fashion icons. Janis Joplin advanced the hippie look with tie-dye and velvet, and the French lithe-hipped beauty and singer Françoise Hardy endorsed Space Age style and was dressed by Paco Rabanne and André Courrèges.

With the 1970s came the flamboyant glam-rock style of David Bowie, with his heavily made-up alter egos Ziggy Stardust and Aladdin Sane. Both men and women imitated his androgynous style – the stardust could spread by association too. The glamorous wives of Mick Jagger attained influential star status: Bianca Jagger patronized Yves Saint Laurent and Ossie Clark and was famous for her regular appearances at nightclub Studio 54, while later the Texan model Jerry Hall also came to dominate newspaper headlines. Jagger himself was a flamboyant dresser, and performed in Hyde Park in an androgynous white-frilled top and leather choker. At the same time, the punk band the Sex Pistols were openly used as clothes horses by Vivienne Westwood to promote the punk designs she sold from her London shop.

Madonna was perhaps the most prominent icon of the 1980s, in her low-life corsets and short skirts worn with fishnet tights and strings of rosaries and beads. Jean Paul Gaultier often designed her stage clothes, and she went on to star as the face of Louis Vuitton's advertising campaigns as late as 2009. Streetwear style was brought to the masses when the Beastie Boys launched their album *Licensed To Ill*, and hip hop band Run-DMC made Adidas trainers desirable with their song 'My Adidas'.

The Seattle band Nirvana popularized the grunge look during the following decade, while singer Courtney Love, married to Nirvana's lead singer, Kurt Cobain, became something of a style icon, dressing in glamorous dresses by Versace. When the pop diva Mariah Carey cut the waistband off her jeans, millions of adoring fans followed – what better way to show off a trim midriff and bejewelled navel? Pop princess Gwen Stefani became known for her kookie image, and went further than most by launching her own high-fashion label L.A.M.B. in 2003.

Lisa Armstrong wrote in UK *Vogue* in 2003: 'Fashion and music are now so embedded in one another's cultures that some artists feel that designing clothes is the next logical outlet for their creative impulse.' Certainly the relationship between the two worlds has never been closer. Singer Rihanna starred in a Gucci advertising campaign in 2009, while fashionista Lady Gaga was happy to strut the streets in nothing more than a flesh-coloured body, jacket and heels – one of her frequently outrageous looks. Despite a public battle with drug addiction, Amy Winehouse also spawned a wave of copycat looks with her beehive hair.

Post-1990s hip hop stars such as Lil' Kim have popularized a high-glam look, and numerous hip hop performers have launched their own fashion brands, notably Kimora Lee Simmons with Baby Phat, Sean 'Puff Daddy' Combs with designer label Sean John, and Russell Simmons with Phat Farm. Left Eye of TLC initiated a trend for baseball caps worn with neon clothing, while rap duo Kris Kross encouraged their fans to wear their clothes backwards.

The fashion industry has now learned to surf the waves of the music machine as it rolls on. ∎

TOP: *David Bowie poses in 1974. He was revered for his glam rock style and his stage personas Aladdin Sane and Ziggy Stardust.*

MAIN PICTURE: *Fashion fanatic Lady Gaga performs in full stage get-up in 2008.*

INSET: *Madonna strikes a pose in New York, 1982.*

Mod style inspired Mary Quant, seen here in 1965, to chop off her hair and design neat little mini-dresses. Her look inspired 1960s style as we know it today.

The subculture that inspired 1960s style

IDEA № 62
MODS

The mods were a small subcultural group whose influence spread far beyond their humble beginnings. Although they were British in origin, their distinctive sartorial style – sharp Italian suits for the boys, miniskirts for the girls, short, neat hairstyles for both – soon became an unmistakable look of the early 1960s.

TOP: *Mods pose in Streatham, London, 1976.*

ABOVE: *Phil Daniels and Leslie Ash star in cult mod movie* Quadrophenia, 1979.

At the end of the 1950s, groups of fashion-minded teens and 20-some-things in London and southern England coalesced, cutting their hair in sharp French styles, saving up their wages for neatly tailored Italian-style clothing, and riding Italian scooters. Their style was modernist, and from this their title 'mod' was derived. It was essential to look stylish and perfectly groomed. The boys favoured expensive suits, Fred Perry shirts and pointed shoes; the girls flaunted their figures in daringly short skirts and tight hipster trousers. The mods wanted to consume. They were earning money and wanted to show it off – this was the first postwar generation that had not only a disposable income but also the opportunity to spend it on nightclubs, music, scooters and clothes.

Although they became famed for peppering their clothing with badges and for customizing their scooters with multiple mirrors, the early mods were minimalists at heart. When they wore big green hooded parkas on their scooters, it was to protect their precious suits from the dirt of the open road.

By 1962 the media had started reporting on the mod look and lifestyle. Amphetamines kept the mods dancing all night, and new mod pop groups emerged. But by 1964 the newspaper headlines were more often about mod violence than mod style. Mods and rockers – their leather-clad rivals – clashed violently in brawls in Brighton and other southern English seaside towns, scenes that would later be depicted in the 1979 cult film *Quadrophenia*.

The mods inspired the designer Mary Quant to produce neat little mini-dresses and to **sport** a sharp Vidal Sassoon five-point haircut; mod suits started to be mass-produced. When they adopted their small-collared, tight-trousered suits, the Beatles at once immortalized the style, and it moved into mainstream fashion. But the look faded in popularity as swiftly as it had grown. Though there was a mod revival in the UK in the late 1970s, by 1966 most of the original mods had grown up, got married or become so dis-illusioned by the commercial hijacking of their style that they had simply moved on. But their influence remained – not least in the way they inspired the designs of Mary Quant, one of the driving forces behind 1960s style. ∎

*Punk-inspired wedding dress by
designer Zandra Rhodes, 1979.*

From sidewalk to catwalk

IDEA № 63

INFLUENTIAL STREET FASHION

The elegant ladies who shopped at Dior were appalled when Yves Saint Laurent introduced references from biker and beat subcultures for his 1960 Beat collection for Christian Dior. Why should they pay high prices for street fashion, even if it was reworked in luxurious crocodile and mink?

Yet Saint Laurent's finely crafted black leather jackets, turtleneck jumpers and helmet-style hats marked the start of what would be a long-standing symbiotic relationship between the street and the designer.

Previously it was mainstream fashion that had reworked the trends and silhouettes set by the designers, but this time it was the other way around – street fashion had influenced a leading **couture** house. American *Vogue* disapproved, commenting that the collection was designed for youthful women 'who expect to change the line with frequency and rapidity, and who are possessed of superb legs and slim, young, goddess figures'. But the world of couture was about to get a sharp wake-up call. Youth fashion and miniskirts were set to dominate the next decade, and many young designers were to reject couture as stuffy and old-fashioned.

After 1960, subcultural fashion and street style continued to have a major impact on the catwalk. When Saint Laurent opened his own fashion house in 1961, he offered his clients a new take on the existentialists of the Left Bank. Mary Quant borrowed from the **mods**; Bill Gibb drew references from the **hippies** in their kaftans; Zandra Rhodes took on **punk**, accessorizing expensive dresses with safety pins. During the 1980s, Commes des Garçons and Yohji Yamamoto took that punk and skinhead staple, the Dr. Martens boot, and raised it to high fashion, starting a mainstream craze for the shoes and boots. Fast-forward to the 1990s, and designers continued to regurgitate their different versions of subcultural movements: Marc Jacobs with **grunge**, Chanel with surfer style, Rifat Ozbek with the Rasta look.

International designers regularly send their scouts down to London markets such as Portobello and Brick Lane, in order to bring street fashion influences back to the drawing board. But unlike those early Dior-clad women, today's ready-to-wear and couture clients are thoroughly happy about it. ∎

Dress by Givenchy for Spring/
Summer 2010. The black-and-
white graphic motifs of Op art
continue to inspire designers.

Straight out of the gallery

IDEA № 64
OP AND POP ART

The term Op art was coined in the early 1960s to describe an art movement that focused on contrasting lines and patterns that played games with human perception. Pop art, which emerged in London and New York in 1960, celebrated consumerism and pop culture, and was led by artists such as Roy Lichtenstein, Jasper Johns and Andy Warhol.

The graphic modern look of Op art was exactly what young people wanted. Larry Aldrich, an art collector and dress manufacturer, printed dresses inspired by the graphic Op art style of the painter Bridget Riley, without her knowledge. Riley eventually sued Aldrich, but it was too late to stop the imagery from her paintings being imitated, and between 1963 and 1966 not only fashion but numerous upholstery and wallpaper designs were inspired by Riley. Even Mary Quant designed a black-and-white striped Op art suit in 1966.

Some Op artists decided to produce fashion goods themselves. The Italian painter Getulio Alviani worked with the designer Germana Marucelli to produce Op-printed sheath dresses and long pleated silk gowns. He went on to collaborate with the American designer Rudi Gernreich, to create a provocative swimsuit in 1966 made from strips of adhesive tape stretched in a V from the shoulders to the crotch.

Andy Warhol produced silk-screen printed dresses and shirts bearing images from his artworks such as Brillo boxes and S & H Green Stamps. Other fashion designers used Pop art as inspiration for their collections, such as Yves Saint Laurent with printed comic-strip dresses, Pierre Cardin with arresting red vinyl coats and Halston with dresses printed with Warhol-inspired flowers.

During the 1980s, artist Keith Haring, known for his bold graffiti-inspired Pop art paintings, opened a New York store called Pop Shop, where he sold, among other things, T-shirts and badges bearing his images. In 1983 he moved further into fashion and collaborated with Vivienne Westwood for her Witches collection, for which she reproduced his artwork on printed fabrics in fluorescent colours. In 2003, Japanese artist Takashi Murakami, known for his own Pop style called Superflat, began a collaboration with Marc Jacobs at Louis Vuitton, starting with a new multicoloured monogram for Vuitton followed by limited-edtion handbags in 2007. Murakami's bright colours and cartoon-style aesthetic breathed new life into the range of accessories. Jacobs explained in *Women's Wear Daily*: 'I wanted everything to be joyous.'

During the 1990s Versace created a dress covered in screen-printed heads of Marilyn Monroe, paying homage to Andy Warhol. The master of Pop and self-promotion may be long gone, but his legacy lives on. Warhol's fame, at least, has lasted for longer than the prescribed 15 minutes. ∎

TOP: *Yves Saint Laurent's striking dresses of 1966 act as a canvas for Pop art images by Andy Warhol.*

ABOVE: *Andy Warhol's legacy lives on with this dress designed by Gianni Versace, worn here by Naomi Campbell in 1991.*

A short, sharp shock

IDEA № 65
THE MINI

Daring short skirts exposing acres of leg were an exciting proposition for young women of the 1960s, and they could not get enough of them. Never had so much leg been revealed in public. By 1965 miniskirts had reached mid-thigh, and still they crept further up. Their shock value is hard to overestimate.

While designers such as André Courrèges and John Bates had introduced short skirts in the early 1960s, it is Mary Quant who should be remembered as the true progenitor of the miniskirt. Inspired by the **mods** with their neat, geometric tailoring and Italian-influenced dress, Quant produced minidresses to sell at her King's Road boutique, Bazaar. The pinafore dresses and short, brightly coloured skirts were, crucially for the fashionable 1960s girls who wore them, worlds apart from the voluptuous New Look style that had entranced their mothers.

Quant's ever-shorter designs were said to have made 'whole countries' gasp with outrage and reluctant admiration. 'Everybody knows how dramatically Mary skittled the staid old fuddy-duddy fashion industry,' said *Vanity Fair* in 1971. Many were outraged by what they saw as common indecency. Coco Chanel denounced miniskirts as disgusting. And Cecil Beaton opined: 'Never in the history of fashion has so little material been raised so high to reveal so much that needs to be covered up so badly.'

Short skirts resurfaced again during the 1980s, with designers such as Azzedine Alaïa producing tight curva-ceous minis; and a black miniskirt worn with opaque **tights** became the standard uniform for young working women.

And so the short skirt drifts in and out of fashion, without ever quite going away. Whether worn in flared, ruched, stretch or puffball form, the mini is here to stay. ∎

TOP: *Jungle-print minidress, 1967.*

ABOVE: *Mary Quant, the Brit who ensured the popularity of the mini, poses here in 1967.*

Twiggy shows a bit of leg for British Vogue, July 1967.

'Quant's ever-shorter designs were said to have made whole countries gasp with outrage'

When legs became the new erogenous zones

IDEA № 66

TIGHTS

As miniskirts grew shorter through the 1960s, creeping inexorably up the thigh, the invention of tights must have been a relief to many girls. They no longer had to rely on stockings and suspenders, and they could once again run for a bus without fear of flashing their knickers.

The new opaque tights in bright colours were the perfect partners for the short skirts of the 1960s.

Indeed, it was probably only because of the thick tights that could be worn with them that skirts reached their shortest ever, in 1969, with the micro-mini. Tights revolutionized the way women moved in skirts or shorts, and allowed the long-limbed to show off their assets to the maximum – the legs were the new erogenous zones.

Ribbed woollen tights became available in the early 1960s in Europe, while sheer **nylon** stockings attached to a heavy denier pant (known as panty-hose) came into the shops in the USA. It was the freezing winter of 1963 that inspired some women to ditch their stockings and opt for tights or panty-hose instead.

In 1965 Pierre Cardin was one of the first fashion designers to offer women tights. They were thick, opaque and monochrome in bright colours for winter, and white or patterned for summer. In the same year Mary Quant launched her collection of tights in myriad colours, while Emilio Pucci offered versions covered with his signature swirl prints. Other late-1960s trends included hosiery with diamond patterns, fishnets, and tights in deep natural tan. Tights were initially slow to filter into the mainstream, but by the 1970s most women were choosing

tights or pantyhose for their convenience and comfort, and stockings accounted for only 5 percent of the market.

During the late 1970s the **punk**s realized that ripped and torn fishnet tights would make a shocking impact, particularly when teamed with black stilettos. But by the 1980s women wanted more feminine, sexy tights, so they opted for lacy hosiery, fishnets and dark or black opaque tights worn with tight miniskirts. In the 1990s women enthusiastically embraced a new development: control tights, which – rather like stretch corsetry – were designed to mould the stomach and buttocks towards curvaceous perfection. Liberating, figure-enhancing and practical, what would the modern woman do without tights? ■

MAIN PICTURE: *Actress Daryl Hannah models sheer hosiery in 1999.*

INSET: *A provocative Pretty Polly advertisement, 1970s.*

For the first time, tough tights that don't look it.

PP
PRETTY POLLY
STOCKINGS 15

'Tights revolutionized the way women moved in skirts or shorts, and allowed the long-limbed to show off their assets'

Pioneering designer André
Courrèges, famed for his
all-white collection, shows
reversible pink and white
gabardine outfits worn
over shorts in 1965.

Fashion's futuristic pioneers

IDEA № 67
SPACE AGE

As the Space Race gathered pace in the mid-1960s, with the American and Soviet superpowers obsessively intent on chalking up firsts in space exploration, so the hip young things slung on their flat white boots, short tabard dresses, catsuits and helmets. The Space Race was in full flow, and everyone was going NASA-crazy.

French designer and ex-civil engineer André Courrèges launched his 1964 Space Age collection in an all-white chrome-trimmed showroom. His geometric-cut clothes were uncompromisingly heavy and hung away from the body, giving them a life of their own. The look may not have been universally loved, but a pair of Courrèges-style white boots became one of the iconic accessories of the decade. 'Can one show oneself in the street dressed in creations designed for the year 2000?' asked *Vogue*.

Pierre Cardin followed with his 1967 Cosmocorps collection of belted tabard dresses and zip jackets for men, and even went on to design spacesuits for NASA in 1970. And the innovative Paco Rabanne was not content with dresses of fabric or even leather – his were intergalactic chain-mail concoctions in plastic or metal. He called his first haute **couture** collection of 1966 'Twelve Unwearable Dresses'. Numerous other designers embraced the new Space Age look, celebrating their diverse visions of the future by experimenting with new materials: Mary Quant with PVC macs; Betsey Johnson with cheeky frocks in sheer plastic; and Pierre Cardin with his newly developed fabric Cardine, for taut dresses that hung away from the body as if they were moulded rather than stitched.

The Space Age aesthetic has continued long after the 1960s. Issey Miyake played with new textiles and silhouettes in the 1980s, developing bamboo, paper and plastic, and casting breastplates from laminated polyester. In the 1990s Helmut Lang decorated shift dresses with holograms and reflective stripes. Contemporary British designer Hussein Chalayan continued to test the boundaries of fashion and technology, in 2007 producing fabric combining Swarovski crystals and flickering LED lights – and for the ultimate party trick, dresses made of aircraft materials that changed shape by remote control. ∎

Hussein Chalayan's avant-garde Spring/Summer 2007 show included futuristic dresses that changed shape on the catwalk using computer technology. The skirt shown here (top and above) widens, and the hat has a shrinking brim.

The Terrible Trio break the mould

IDEA № 68

RAW PHOTOGRAPHY

In the 1960s fashion photography was redefined by a trio of London photographers: David Bailey, Brian Duffy and Terence Donovan. Until then fashion photography had presented aspirational images of a rarefied, high-class world. These three photographers broke the mould with their sexually charged, documentary-style photographs.

Their pictures were honest and raw, shot in high contrast on grainy film, and influenced by French New Wave cinema. Models were portrayed as attainable real women, rather than impossible mannequins on pedestals, untouchable and refined in their tight poses. And the backdrops for the pictures were no longer elegant drawing-rooms; these working-class rebels preferred to go back to their roots, shooting the girls in London's gritty East End, celebrating its dirty streets and industrial backdrops as if in a documentary photograph.

Society photographer Norman Parkinson dubbed them the Black Trinity and *The Sunday Times* called them the Terrible Trio for their defiant break with the accepted notions of glamour. Bailey, Duffy and Donovan were proudly working class, heterosexual and irreverent, cast in a different mould from their effete society predecessors such as Cecil Beaton. Despite their working-class roots, they moved with a fashionable, chic set of actors, artists, musicians and **celebrities**, gaining celebrity status themselves. Bailey, for example, photographed the wedding of East End gangster Reggie Kray, and was himself married to the actress Catherine Deneuve and then model Marie Helvin.

Rather than treating models as clothes-hangers for the latest trends, they tried to capture the girls' personalities, and the relationship between a woman and her clothes. *The Times* commented: 'Bailey quickly stirred up the fashion department at *Vogue*, where, in the early Sixties, the implicit sexuality of his photographs was at odds with the prevailing style of tight, well-behaved polish.'

Bailey, Duffy and Donovan's irreverent and lively photographs mirrored the energetic new fashion scene of Swinging London, with its focus on youth and consumerism. Their work was hugely in demand from *Vogue*, *Elle* and scores of other fashion magazines and newspapers throughout the decade and afterwards. Their legacy lives on, with informally posed photographs still appearing in magazines – although, in contrast, today's models are airbrushed to an almost robotic perfection. ∎

TOP: *A model wearing a dress by Laura for Joan Arkin poses with British band Blossom Toes on a London street in 1968. The new fashion photography was gritty, urban and informal.*

ABOVE: *Brian Duffy photographs a* Vogue *shoot in action.*

'They were proudly working class, heterosexual and irreverent, cast in a different mould from their effete society predecessors'

*Movie star Evan Rachel Wood flaunts
her tattoo at the 2009 Oscars.*

TOP: *Temporary tattoos by Chanel for Spring/Summer 2010. These were a short-lived product.*

ABOVE: *Dramatic tattoo effects at the Jean Paul Gaultier couture show for Spring/Summer 2008.*

Body art goes mainstream

IDEA Nº 69
TATTOOS

Traditionally, tattoos were the preserve of sailors and criminals, and definitely of men; it was not until the late twentieth century that the tattoo as a fashion statement for women became acceptable.

Human beings have always liked to decorate their bodies. The famous Ötzi the Iceman, whose perfectly preserved body, dating back to c. 3300 BCE, was discovered in 1991, had more than 50 tattoos. The future King Edward VII of Britain had a Jerusalem Cross tattooed on his arm, sparking a trend among the British aristocracy. Winston Churchill's mother, Lady Randolph Churchill, was said to have had a tattoo of a snake around her wrist, though this is no more than a rumour, and it certainly would not have been shown in public.

Tattoos bridged the gap between decorative clothing, jewellery and make-up, and added a new dimension to late twentieth-century women's dress. Rock stars of the 1960s such as Joan Baez were forerunners of the trend. Janis Joplin had a wrist tattoo and a small heart emblazoned on her breast. By degrees tattoos for women became more socially acceptable, and by the 1990s every supermodel, actress and 20-something fashionista worth her salt sported a tattoo. The Brazilian model Gisele had a small star on her wrist and the actress Winona Ryder acquired a delicate S-shaped tat on one forearm.

The new tattoos were frequently monochrome and usually discreet – on wrists, ankles or lower back – so that they could be hidden with clothing or jewellery when needed. For those unwilling to take the plunge, both adhesive tattoos and henna-painted designs provided a popular, pain-free and forgivingly temporary alternative.

On the catwalk, Jean Paul Gaultier put real and fake tattoos under tattoo-print chiffon clothing for his Spring/Summer 1994 collection, and revisited the tattoo print again for 2009. John Galliano designed tattoo-print body stockings for Christian Dior in 2004. Some people even used well-known brands as tattoos: 'Not only do dozens of Nike employees have a swoosh tattooed on their calves, but tattoo parlours all over North America report that the swoosh has become their most popular item. Human branding?' wrote Naomi Klein in *No Logo* (2000). Chanel launched sets of temporary transfer tattoos in 2010, based on interlinked chain motifs, and Louis Vuitton followed with tattoos of its signature monogram in 2011.

And for those who merely want to enhance their looks, tattoos can merge with cosmetics in the form of permanent make-up. Colour is carefully tattooed onto the face to give the impression of lip-liner, lipstick or eyeliner. A cosmetically tattooed woman need never be without her make-up again. ∎

Light as air, fashion's new finery

IDEA № 70
THE DELICATE KNIT DRESS

The term knitwear no longer just conjures up chunky jumpers and frumpy twinsets. Thanks to a new breed of designers, fine yarn has been worked into show-stopping red-carpet dresses, ethereal kaftans and even sparkling bikinis.

When husband and wife team Ottavio Missoni and Rosita Jelmini joined forces to found the ready-to-wear knitwear firm Missoni in 1953, no one could have guessed they were to make such a major impact on the fashion industry. The breakthrough came in 1962, when they boldly took an obscure knitting-machine, previously used only to make shawls, and used it to manufacture fine knitted dresses from synthetic and natural yarn.

Missoni's delicate knitwear came coloured and patterned in rainbow stripes, geometric shapes and abstract florals. It was the bright, painterly colours that impressed buyers world-wide, and the press was instantly enthralled. The Missoni collections single-handedly revived an enthusiasm for knitwear. And the designers caused a scandal when they allowed their models to walk the catwalk braless. 'Missoni is in the lead with one of the most sinful dresses among those inspired by Art Deco,' was the judgement of *Women's Wear Daily*.

The designers Julien Macdonald and Lainey Keogh took the delicate knit dress a step further during the 1990s, with their luxury cobweb and feather-weight crochet knits. Karl Lagerfeld had spotted Macdonald at the Royal College of Art in London, scooped him up, and asked him to design the knitwear at Chanel while he was still a student. Macdonald went on to launch his own label, which included exquisite knitted evening dresses in bright colours. British *Vogue* commented: 'Cobwebby, intricate and light as air, Julien Macdonald's knitted dresses are irresistible.' When the buxom British model Kelly Brook arrived at a film premiere bursting out of a clinging pink knitted Macdonald dress (with matching pink knickers) the paparazzi went wild.

Between them, these designers helped to dramatically alter the fashion industry's attitude to knitwear as a lowly product, proving that it can be beautiful, dressy and delicate. As Julien Macdonald said in *Elle*: 'I wanted to show that being a knitwear designer is not just about jumpers.' ∎

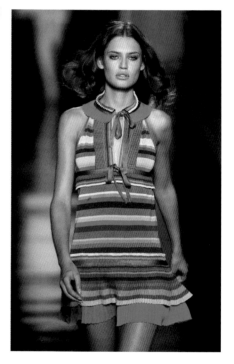

ABOVE: *Fine-knit striped dress with pleat detailing by Missoni for Spring/Summer 2006.*

OPPOSITE: *A model clad in Missoni's cobweb-fine knitwear reclines on pillows in 1975.*

'Missoni's delicate knitwear came coloured and patterned in rainbow stripes, geometric shapes and abstract florals'

ABOVE LEFT TO RIGHT:
Beige, black and white bonded fibre paper dress by the Scott Paper Company, 1966.

Short sleeveless red paper dress, c. 1967.

Black and white spotted paper dress by the Waste Basket Boutique, 1967.

Printed orange, pink and purple paper dress made from bonded cellulose fibre by Dipso, 1967.

MAIN PICTURE: *Disposable blue and green printed paper dress, 1967.*

'Dresses and underwear made out of synthetic paper became the ultimate in 1960s chic'

Throwaway clothing for a new age

IDEA № 71
DISPOSABLE FASHION

One of the youth trends of the Swinging Sixties was the indulgent habit of quick-fix fashion – buying the latest hip garment, wearing it and throwing it away. Such behaviour was in complete contrast to the meticulous hoarding mentality of the war generation and brought with it a heady sense of freedom, progress and leaving the past behind.

Wonderland was the result of a collaboration between Helen Storey and Professor Tony Ryan, and was conceived as a series of disappearing dresses made from textiles that slowly dissolve in water.

The 1960s saw a boom in the production of cheap synthetic fabrics, and a short-lived, but major, trend for clothes made out of paper emerged. The Scott Paper Company had first produced paper clothing as a marketing gimmick in the United States in 1966. Dresses and underwear made out of the synthetic paper called Tyvek became the ultimate in 1960s chic, and paper-clothing boutiques sprang up. Dispo launched paper garments bearing swirling psychedelic prints, and fashion designers Betsey Johnson and Zandra Rhodes made paper dresses for their up-market clientele.

Even the artists and poets joined in – Andy Warhol with a paper dress printed with his trademark Campbell's soup cans, and Allen Ginsberg with a dress covered in poetry. A paper dress could be easily cut to any length and, amazingly, was tough enough to survive up to five nights on the dancefloor. Soon there were waterproofed paper bikinis and raincoats, paper suits, and even a paper wedding dress.

Several decades later, designer Hussein Chalayan experimented with paper clothing for his graduation collection in 1993, and during the 1990s Issey Miyake recycled pleated rice-paper to make a series of delicate dresses. For her Wonderland project of 2008, designer Helen Storey took disposable fashion even further, with plastic dresses of biodegradable polyvinyl alcohol that dissolved on contact with water. 'This is the ultimate in disposable fashion. A symbol of our throwaway society – not to mention the stuff of male fantasies. Here is the world's first dissolvable dress,' wrote Roger Highfield in *The Daily Telegraph* in 2007.

There is, of course, another less attractive side to the concept of fashion as disposable. With high-street retailers such as Primark, Zara, H&M and Topshop retailing clothes for extra-ordinarily low prices, almost everyone can now buy clothes, jettison them and replace them for a pittance. As a result, textile waste is on the rise, and countless tonnes of unwanted cloth-ing end up as landfill each year. Our new love for super-cheap clothes may come at a terrible cost to the planet. ■

'Hippies rejected consumerism and artifice and anything slick or urbane'

A young hippie chills out in Rome in 1970.

Flower power

IDEA № 72
HIPPIES

'Tune in and drop out.' 'Make love not war.' These were the mantras of the hippies who emerged in mid-1960s America, promoting sexual liberation, experimenting with psychedelic drugs and expressing their pacifist values by demonstrating against nuclear weapons and the Vietnam War.

ABOVE LEFT: *Singer and hippie icon Janis Joplin, with her rich silks, tassels and sheepskin, proves that hippie style can also be luxurious.*

ABOVE: *Vanessa Redgrave goes for the full luxury hippie look in 1976.*

With an interest in ecology and craft-based or multi-ethnic fashion, they instigated a new dress code for a generation.

Between 1965 and 1967, young beatniks gathered on the coast of California, and became known as hippies, derived from the word 'hip', or up to date. They were worried about getting drafted to Vietnam, sickened by the soulless consumerism that they saw surrounding them, and concerned about the environment. Ardently keen on getting back to nature, many dropped out of mainstream society in order to form communes. Haight-Ashbury in San Francisco became a centre of the movement, and the summer of 1967 saw a peak of as many as 100,000 people gathering there in what was known as the Summer of Love. After this, the hippie style and philosophy spread quickly across the rest of America, and would go on to expand its influence around the world.

The hippie look appealed to those who wanted something other than the mod-style miniskirts and slick short haircuts of the early 1960s.

Unlike their predecessors, hippies rejected consumerism and artifice and anything slick or urbane.

Instead they borrowed from foreign cultures. In their search for spiritual enlightenment, many travelled to spend time in the ashrams of India, or simply embraced Eastern value systems and therapies. Through this fascination with the East numerous oriental references found their way into hippie fashions. They wore loose, layered clothing in bright Indian silks, and teamed flared **jeans** with thick Afghan sheepskin coats and embroidered or fringed jackets. Long hair dressed with flowers, headbands and strings of beads finished off the look – for both women and men. And for the jetset who preferred expensive hotels to overland travel, but wanted the hippie look, designer Yves Saint Laurent was on hand to provide printed calico smocks and luxury patchwork with a high price tag, while Zandra Rhodes offered voluminous printed chiffon dresses.

With the end of the Vietnam War in 1975, the movement somewhat lost its focus. It was time to make way for the **punk**s, who were as confrontational as the hippies were peaceful.

The impact that the hippie movement has had on late twentieth- and early twenty-first-century fashion is enormous. Designers repeatedly return to dip into the hippie archive for inspiration – from the long, flowing silhouettes, to the prints and homespun detailing. Dolce & Gabbana played with patchwork and beads in 1993. Tom Ford for Gucci offered feathered jeans and bold floral patterns in 1999. Anna Sui offered folksy floral prints in 2008 and an urban hippie look complete with suede tassels and patterned **tights** for 2010. In the world of fashion at least, the Summer of Love still lives on. ∎

A bejewelled pierced belly button was the height of chic during the 1990s.

From tongue studs to belly-button rings

BODY PIERCING

Humans have pierced various body parts since time immemorial. Piercing was used to signify strength among Roman centurions, as an initiation ritual among the American Indians, and to denote royalty for the ancient Egyptians. Even the otherwise prudish Victorians are thought to have been partial to nipple-piercing.

Drew Barrymore arrives at a film premiere in 2009 and shows off her new pierced tongue.

Of course, women had pierced their earlobes for centuries. But it was not until as recently as the 1990s that piercings elsewhere on the body became acceptable to mainstream society in the West.

When, in the 1960s, the American **hippies** returned home after travelling to India, some sported pierced noses inspired by the bejewelled nasal piercings of Indian women, for whom they were a mark of beauty and social standing. Gradually other Westerners started to copy the look, especially among the various subcultural youth 'tribes'. The **punk**s used body piercing to shock, running studs and pins through eyebrows, cheeks and lips, while by the 1980s a pierced nose was part of a goth's essential uniform. But it was the 1990s when nipples, tongues, eyebrows and navels regularly became sacrificed to the piercing gun. Supermodel Christy Turlington began to flaunt a bejewelled belly button, and a navel piercing thus became the latest fashion look to complement a pair of low-slung hipster **jeans**.

At the end of the twentieth century, with fashion trends ebbing and flowing at whiplash speed, and consumerism at its height, for some people piercings provided a sense of permanence and authenticity. Piercings could still symbolize a rite of passage, or a sense of belonging to a certain group or style tribe. And for those who just wanted to get the look there were magnetic chin studs, clip-on nipple rings and stick-on nose studs all available at the click of a mouse over **the Internet.** ∎

'Piercings could still symbolize a rite of passage, or a sense of belonging to a certain group or style tribe'

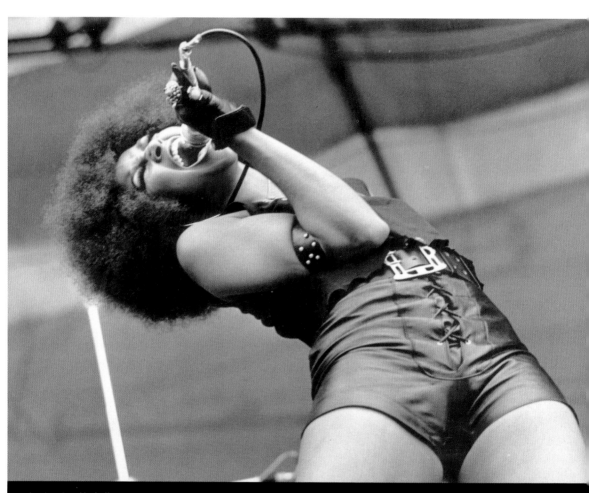

American singer Marsha Hunt works it for the crowd in raunchy hot pants, 1969.

'Big Afro hair, hot pants and bold make-up and jewellery completed the look'

Fashion gets into the groove

IDEA № 74
FUNK

ABOVE: *Singers The Three Degrees flaunt their funky style – crotch-hugging flares and big hair – in 1974.*

BELOW: *Dancers in the USA, 1974. The girl sports platform shoes and a glossy pair of blue trousers with matching shirt.*

The African–American slang word 'funk' originally meant something that smelled pungent, or more particularly of sexual intercourse. In the early twentieth century it was applied principally to black funk music, which had a mellow and syncopated rhythm suggestive of the sexual act. The distinctive dress styles of various funk artists were keenly followed by their fans.

James Brown was one of the first artists to become known for his distinct funk sound. The African–American funk music of the 1960s and 1970s with its driving bass lines, was a fusion of soul, jazz and R&B, played by Sly and the Family Stone, Bootsy Collins and George Clinton. Funk also came to be associated with radical black politics.

The roots of funk dressing lie in the black ghettoes of America, where the successful wore highly flamboyant clothes to advertise their riches in their own way – one that did not conform to white society's values. They combined flares with close-fitting shirts, hats with gold chain bands and big gold jewellery. The funk dress code was all about sex and money. Flared trousers drew the eye down to the flapping fabric, but also drew attention to the tight area around the crotch. Tom Wolfe wrote: 'They're into the James Brown look, they're into the ruffled shirts ... looking sharp.'

For the girls, the funk look was about showing off a body both beautiful and provocative in high platform shoes and slinky dresses or flares. Satin and lamé jumpsuits and glittery make-up made an impact on-stage. Big Afro hair, **hot pants**, bold make-up and jewellery completed the look. Blaxploitation films of the early 1970s, such as *Shaft* and *Super Fly*, immortalized the look and introduced funk style to a much wider audience.

The look was indisputably carried off by urban African–Americans better than their white counterparts. The 'funky chic' look spread from black to white culture in New York, Los Angeles and San Francisco, and on to Europe. But the white adaptation of the funk look was more toned down and less erotic and ostentatious. Funk, together with the psychedelic movement, went on to inspire the **glam** looks adopted by David Bowie and Gary Glitter at the end of the decade. ∎

Wear them if you dare

Sex symbol Catherine Bach plays Daisy Duke in The Dukes of Hazzard. *Denim hot pants became known as Daisy Dukes.*

IDEA № 75

HOT PANTS

Hot pants were immortalized in song by soul legend James Brown in 1971, but they were not new. Marlene Dietrich wore hot pants in *The Blue Angel* in 1930 in her role as a club singer, and these daringly brief shorts had been associated with cabaret and prostitutes until they appeared on European streets in the late 1960s.

By 1971, hot pants as mainstream fashion had spread to North America. Along with the micromini, they were the most revealing piece of clothing a woman could wear on the lower part of her body in public – away from the beach.

It was *Women's Wear Daily* that coined the name 'hot pants' for these briefest of brief shorts. They were a natural progression from the 1960s miniskirt, which had grown increasingly and indecently short. Mary Quant designed hot pants in the late 1960s, and minimal shorts appeared on the catwalk in Paris by André Courrèges and Christian Dior. The style soon filtered down to mainstream street fashion, in leather, denim and wool for day, and velvet and satin for night. Often worn over thick coloured **tights**,

they were teamed with mid-calf low-heeled go-go boots or platform wedges.

Southwest Airlines of Texas even adopted hot pants for its flight attendants, while during the 1970s the baseball team the Philadelphia Phillies employed a group of hot-pant-wearing usherettes, known as the Hot Pants Patrol, around their stadium. In 1971 those in hot pants were even allowed access to the Royal Enclosure at Ascot Racecourse, with its strict dress code, but only if the overall outfit was deemed satisfactory.

During the 1980s female hip-hop groups and rappers such as Salt-N-Pepa wore hot pants with bomber jackets, outsize earrings and long fake nails. In denim, hot pants became known as 'Daisy Dukes', thanks to the hot-pant-clad sex-bomb played by Catherine

Bach in the television series *The Dukes of Hazzard* (1979–85). A decade later they became popular again, partly influenced by the action-film and computer-game character Lara Croft.

But for many, hot pants will be best remembered for the pair in gold lamé that barely covered the perfect buttocks of Kylie Minogue in the video for her 2000 hit single 'Spinning Around'. Hot pants helped to relaunch her career. ∎

Bowie fans flaunt their hot pants in 1973.

'Marc Bolan dabbled with women's
evening wear, opting for clinging costumes in
sequins, Lurex and satin'

Glitter, glitz and glamour for the boys

IDEA № 76

GLAM

In the 1970s glam rock gave men a chance to dress up like women and flaunt their finery and feathers. With its glitter suits, make-up and heels, this was one of the few times during the twentieth century that fashion challenged preconceived notions of masculinity.

While **hippies** had embraced unisex dressing, they looked downbeat and celebrated a return to nature. Glam fans rejected the homespun and delighted in outrageous style and artifice, taking inspiration from science fiction and 1930s Hollywood films.

The extraordinary stage costumes of David Bowie spearheaded this outbreak of camp drama, which found popularity mainly in Britain. Together with Marc Bolan, the extrovert lead singer of T. Rex, and members of such bands as Sweet, Roxy Music, Slade and The Glitter Band, Bowie adopted platform heels, flamboyant make-up and highly theatrical clothing. Gary Glitter always performed in high platform boots. When Mick Jagger took to the stage in London's Hyde Park in 1969, he dared to wear a leather choker festooned with studs, a frilled tunic top and white flares. Marc Bolan meanwhile dabbled with women's evening wear, opting for clinging costumes in sequined Lurex and satin, with an infamous feather boa for that final showgirl touch.

David Bowie as Ziggy Stardust dyed his hair in bright colours, and was celebrated for his extreme stage make-up. By 1973 he had spawned both male and female Ziggy clones, who flocked to his concerts in costume; some even flaunted their sparkling futuristic outfits on the street during the day. Bowie daringly claimed, in a 1972 interview in *Melody Maker*, that he was bisexual. 'For all his "fag" image, nowhere is he more loved than in traditionally "earthy" working class cities like Glasgow, Liverpool, Leeds ... All across the country on his last tour, boys and girls, men and women were turning up in their Bowie make-up and garb,' reported *Music Scene* in 1973.

These gender-bender glam kids were paving the way for the **punk**s and the **New Romantics**, who were to continue the party by celebrating artifice, make-up and dressing up for both sexes. ∎

TOP: *Marc Bolan struts his stuff in full glam getup, a gold jumpsuit and white jacket, in 1973.*

ABOVE: *Mick Jagger performs at Hyde Park, London, in 1969, wearing a studded leather choker, white flares and a white tunic top.*

'Halston's kaftans, shift dresses, shirt dresses, tunics and wide-legged trousers embodied everything that the elegant modern woman craved'

Sleek, chic and feline: the new seventies simplicity

IDEA Nº 77

LOW-KEY LUXURY

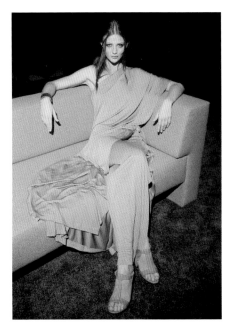

ABOVE: *The signature languid lines and soft elegance of this 2009 Halston dress look strong and modern while continuing the 1970s aesthetic.*

OPPOSITE: *This elegant 1972 dress by Halston combines glamour with comfort and, crucially, looks effortless.*

By the 1970s, the independent woman required a simple, practical wardrobe – and the United States was the country to give it to her, with an elegant, no-frills approach to dressing incorporating fluid lines, simple cuts and lengths of durable fabric.

New York had developed into an exciting artistic centre, and America became known for its sophisticated ready-to-wear collections, which were neither Paris **couture**, nor mass-manufactured high-street styles. This was new, relaxed, luxurious off-the-peg clothing.

Roy Halston Frowick, or Halston as he was known, was a true all-American designer. After working as a milliner, he launched his own ready-to-wear line in 1966, combining comfort and glamour with a relaxed **sport**y style. His kaftans, shift dresses, shirt dresses, tunics and wide-legged trousers embodied everything that the elegant modern woman craved. 'Halston's proportions were perfect. His clothes followed the shape of a woman's body without being tight; they held the body while still retaining a certain languor,' explained Grace Mirabella in Steven Bluttal's book *Halston* (2001).

Fellow designer Geoffrey Beene continued this low-key approach– keeping clothes striking and elegant in black and white, while minimizing accessories. Beene made his name with simple suits in jersey, flannel and wool. He designed sequin dresses inspired by American football shirts, and used long zips in bright colours as decorative devices. Bill Blass was another master

of American daywear, with his frilled dresses and careful tailoring, highlighted with discreet detail or trim in a flash of bright colour. Marketing geniuses and designers Ralph Lauren and Calvin Klein saw the way to producing luxury everyday clothing for men and women – the beginnings of the fashion empires they were to build in the next 40 years.

Over the water in London, Jean Muir was fulfilling a similar aesthetic, creating relaxed but sophisticated womenswear. She worked with jersey and suede to make carefully cut fluid suits, shawls, and dresses with draw-string waists.

The new designers had proved that fashion could be comfortable and practical, while remaining stylish and modern. ■

IDEA № 78

BLACK IS BEAUTIFUL

TOP: *Model Alek Wek in 2008, promoting Speedo's swimwear line for the World Swim Against Malaria.*

ABOVE: *A black model appears on the cover of American* **Vogue** *for the first time in 1974. Her name was Beverly Johnson.*

It was not until 1974 that a black woman appeared on the cover of American *Vogue*, a fact that seems astonishing today. That cover, featuring the model Beverly Johnson, marked a key point in fashion for black women.

African–American model Donyale Luna had appeared on the cover of British *Vogue* in 1966, but it would be another decade before black women were truly accepted by the Western fashion industry.

'If the political protests of the 1960s forced America's eyes open to the undeniable presence and varied beauty of black people, the '70s consolidated that vision,' wrote Barbara Summers in *Black and Beautiful: How Women of Color Changed the Fashion Industry* (1988). The first women of colour to become influential fashion models included Mounia Orhozemane, Beverly Johnson and Princess Elizabeth of Toro. Iman, the daughter of a Somali diplomat, began her modelling career in *Vogue* in 1976 and went on to become one of the highest-paid models of her time.

Just as Western fashion opened up globally during the 1970s, with designers incorporating influences from different cultures into their collections, so it became more open to using non-Caucasian models. During the 1980s Gianni Versace and Yves Saint Laurent routinely used models of all races to promote their work. The retailer Benetton went much further, deliberately selecting young models of widely differing skin colours. By the 1990s Naomi Campbell had reached the elite ranks of **the supermodel**s, becoming a household name all over the world.

In practice, however, for those working in the fashion industry, colour equality was far from evident. In 2008 Italian *Vogue* made a stand against this inequality by dedicating the complete July issue to black women, using black models for all its shoots. The surprise that this caused clearly demonstrated that the fashion industry is anything but colour-blind. The fashion photographer Steven Meisel told the *New York Times* in 2008: 'I have asked my advertising clients so many times, "Can we use a black girl?" They say no.' Naomi Campbell told *Glamour* magazine: 'The American president may be black, but as a black woman, I am still an exception in this business.' Speaking as recently as 2009, she said: 'In the past, there were more opportunities for black models but the trend towards blond women has again become extreme. In magazines, on the catwalk, I see blond, blue-eyed models everywhere.' ∎

British supermodel Naomi Campbell works it for the camera in 1990.

'In 2008 Italian *Vogue* made a stand against this inequality by dedicating a complete issue to black women, using black models for all its shoots'

Rudi Gernreich's unisex thong swimsuits, Los Angeles, USA, 1974.

Daring to bare it on the beach

IDEA № 79
THE THONG

On the beach, the thong looks its best on a perfect body and all-over tan.

The word 'thong' originates from the Old English 'thwong', meaning a flexible leather cord. These rudimentary loin-cloths for men were one of the earliest forms of clothing. The modern thong, however, is thought of mainly as a woman's garment, and was taken up during the twentieth century as beachwear and underwear.

Liberating and provocatively sexy, the thong as we know it was launched in the 1970s, when fashion designer Rudi Gernreich launched his unisex thong swimsuit. Gernreich's background as a dancer inspired him to combine the stretch of leotards and **tights** with a pared-down Bauhaus functionalism in his designs.

Brazilian women were some of the first to take up thong bikinis as swimwear – in Rio very thin versions were known as *fio dental*, or dental floss. By the 1990s thongs were *de rigueur* on American and European beaches.

In the underwear market, the 1980s thong brief, with its strip of fabric that sits between the buttocks, served a useful purpose by diminishing the visible panty line. As low-slung and hip-hugging **jeans** came into fashion in the following decade, the thong would inevitably ride up to be seen above the jeans. This soon became a deliberate

effect, and thongs were designed with feathers, beads and diamanté detailing in order to be shown off.

With their minimal design, thongs reveal a large expanse of buttock. It was reputedly a glimpse of Monica Lewinsky's thong that got President Bill Clinton's pulse racing at the White House, leading him to risk his political career over the illicit affair. In 2010 *Cosmopolitan* magazine declared 'the thong is dead', but on the beaches of Rio this is destined to be ignored. ∎

Sex, studs and safety pins

IDEA № 80
PUNK

When punk first exploded onto the streets in the 1970s, many people were shocked by the appearance of these disaffected youths. Who were these kids with their heavy make-up, tattered clothes and offensive slogans?

London punk, 1981. Bold make-up and customized leathers were all part of the look.

Punk was a surprisingly short-lived cultural phenomenon but it had a major impact, particularly in Britain, and spread to New York, Sydney and around the world. In 1970s Britain the economy was in disarray, unemployment was running high, and many teenagers were bored and restless. British punk was a movement born principally out of angry youth protest. In the summer of 1976 London art students and the unemployed started hanging out on the King's Road in Chelsea, gathering around a shop run by Malcolm McLaren and his fashion designer girlfriend, Vivienne Westwood. The shop – named SEX – sold fetish clothing, bondage trousers, obscene earrings, and deliberately ripped T-shirts featuring in-your-face slogans.

McLaren and Westwood astutely tapped into the psyche of the angry teenager at precisely the right time. In 1976 McLaren founded a band, the Sex Pistols, whom Westwood then dressed in her own designs. With their shocking antics, offensive lyrics and outrageous clothing, the band shot to newspaper prominence, and achieved overnight notoriety as the leaders of noisy, discontented urban youth. McLaren and Westwood were thus a driving force in the creation of the punk movement in Britain, weaving together a winning combination of music and fashion.

Punks wore leather, rubber and PVC. Their clothes were frequently slashed, painted, studded and adorned with safety pins and chains, while hair was often dyed bright, unnatural colours and teased into spikes or a 'mohawk'. Facial piercings were common. Shock value was paramount.

Having emerged as a musical movement independently in the United States and Britain, punk spread throughout Europe. But the moment did not last. By 1979 the Sex Pistols had broken up, their bassist, Sid Vicious, was dead of a heroin overdose and Westwood had moved on to design New Romantic collections. But despite its brevity, punk style left a palpable impact – it showed how fashion could challenge stereotypes of gender and beauty. Punk put London on the map once more as a centre of innovative fashion, and it paved the way for the numerous punk fashion revivals that were to follow. ■

'Punk style showed how fashion could challenge stereotypes of gender and beauty'

Punk pioneers including Chrissie Hynde and Vivienne Westwood pose at the King's Road shop SEX in 1976.

CAD, CAM and 3D scanning

COMPUTER TECHNOLOGY

Life today would be inconceivable without the computer, and it has had a major impact on fashion, from the textile design of a garment, through to its manufacture, marketing and sales. Computer-aided design (CAD) and computer-aided manufacturing (CAM) are now essential tools for the fashion industry.

However, the fashion business was slow to pick up on computer technology. CAD and CAM were not adopted commercially until the early 1970s, when they were used for automated pattern cutting and for grading clothes into sizes, which minimized fabric waste. Computers to control knitting and weaving machinery came next.

It was not until the 1980s that designers started to use computers as part of the creative process, mainly to modify textile prints, as the technology could recreate a print or pattern in a number of different colour schemes quickly and efficiently. Since then, the industry has embraced computer technology for the full design process and for mass-production, particularly for making cheaper clothes in large quantities. The technology improves lead time and overall quality, and as a result new garments can be injected into the high-street stores more quickly – every few weeks, rather than months.

Calvin Klein, Jasper Conran and Ghost started to experiment with CAD, though most high-end fashion designers preferred to use the technology for print rather than garment design. But things are changing with the new generation of designers, reared on computers, who no longer view designing with new technology as soulless or somehow inauthentic. 'We're really on the brink of dramatic change in everything,' predicted Tom Ford in *Women's Wear Daily* in 1999. 'It's all about technology, computers, video conferencing. We're going to live in a more graphic world. It's all about bullet points. Style in the future is going to be the graphics on a computer screen.'

In 1999 Levi's installed a 3D body scanner in its stores. These machines could take a 3D scan of the body and automatically convert it into a pattern for clothing to fit that figure. Was this the future of mass-market **couture**? Computers can also be used to display clothes. In 1998 a Thierry Mugler dress appeared on a 3D animated catwalk, using virtual models, to be watched on a screen. The future might seem a little dull with no shops and no live fashion shows, but new technology is offering exciting new alternatives to the status quo. ∎

A digital hologram model features in a 2007 virtual fashion show by retailer Target.

'New technology is offering exciting
new alternatives'

*Dramatic printed dress by Versace
for Spring/Summer 2001. High-end
designers initially used CAD only
for print design.*

Pirates and posers

IDEA № 82
NEW ROMANTICS

The New Romantics were a small group of London-based posers who originally formed an exciting subcultural tribe during the 1980s. With their extravagant dress and their carefully cultivated sense of style they rapidly influenced the fashion scene, designing clothes, running nightclubs and inspiring the fashion coverage in the hip new magazines *The Face* and *i-D*.

TOP: *New Romantics pose for the camera in London in the 1980s.*

ABOVE: *The New Romantic style encouraged the boys as well as girls to dress up and flaunt their finery.*

When Steve Strange and Rusty Egan designated Tuesday nights as Bowie Nights at a club in London's Soho in 1978, it attracted a new fashion following. Consisting largely of former **punk**s, these were young people who had enjoyed the sartorial aspect of punk but shied away from the movement's violent and anarchistic lifestyle. They formed a glamorous, colourfully dressed crowd, whom the press first dubbed the Blitz Kids (after the Blitz nightclub, a favourite haunt), and then the New Romantics. Other clubs sprang up to cater for the movement's growing popularity, playing music from the new electronic pop/synthesizer bands such as Duran Duran, Adam and the Ants and Spandau Ballet.

New Romantic fashion centred around luxurious fabrics such as velvet, silk and brocade, and a new taste for romantic and flamboyant dress. These self-proclaimed posers took inspiration from both the glamour of the 1930s and the opulence of David Bowie in his Ziggy Stardust phase, finishing off the look with white make-up and deep stripes of coloured blusher on the cheekbones. The boys dressed with the panache of buccaneers, and would happily dress in women's clothing if they felt the urge. The look, in fact, was androgynous: both girls and boys spiked their hair, painted their faces and wore frilled shirts, leggings or voluminous trousers nipped in at the ankle. Pop star Adam Ant popularized his own version of the New Romantic look, dressing as a swashbuckling highwayman, or as a pirate of the high seas. Designers such as Stevie Stewart and David Holah, who went on to form Body Map, offered New Romantic collections. Vivienne Westwood indulged her penchant for the theatrical to the full and toyed with the Regency dandy for her collections, and in 1981 introduced frilled shirts and hussar jackets trimmed with gold braid as part of her Pirates Collection. Romance was far from dead, and the New Romantics and their followers dressed up, went out, and flaunted their pretty new clothes. ∎

'Both girls and boys spiked their hair, painted their faces and wore frilled and ruffled shirts'

Adam Ant wears swashbuckling New Romantic clothes in 1983.

Jock straps and boxer shorts for girls

IDEA № 83

CALVIN KLEIN UNDERWEAR

In 1984 Klein launched boxer shorts for girls complete with a three-button fly, plus a version of the jockstrap with a wide waistband. *Time* magazine called them 'Calvin's New Gender Benders'. Locker-room underwear for women became a sign of the times, a reaction against the push-up Wonderbra and lacy lingerie of the 1980s.

Calvin Klein had first launched his men's shorts and briefs with a branded elastic waist in 1982. They were brilliantly marketed. Bruce Weber's stunning photographs of a well-endowed Olympic pole-vaulter, shot erotically from below, ensured good sales of these simple cotton shorts bearing a designer price tag.

The success of Klein's suggestive ads of girls wearing the underwear while pulling off their T-shirts to just skim the nipple, proved once again that sex sells. Sales rocketed. Klein said: 'I think there's something incredibly sexy about a woman wearing her boyfriend's T-shirt and underwear.' In 1992, Klein pushed the limits even further, by using a topless Kate Moss, and a half-naked rap musician, Marky Mark, to promote his underwear. Overnight, sales increased by a third, and many stores quickly sold out.

Klein had timed his underwear launch well, cleverly tapping into the 1980s obsession with designer labels, andthe enthusiasm for **sport** and the gym. Men allowed the branded elasticated waistband to be seen when wearing low-slung **jeans**, using their underwear as another way to flaunt a designer logo. For women the style was athletic, straightforward and strangely sexy in a new fresh way, with a unisex, androgynous style that also chimed in well with the pending 1990s minimalist aesthetic. Klein had successfully set the tone for the new decade. And of course other brands such as Fila and Sloggi soon followed with their own versions. ∎

Striking a pose in black Calvin Kleins.

Gisele Bündchen models
Calvin Klein underwear.

Flygirls and B-boys take centre stage

IDEA № 84

HIP HOP

In the 1980s a vibrant new street culture emerged from the African–American, Caribbean–American and Latino youth of New York's South Bronx. It centred around breakdancing, rap music and graffiti art. Spreading swiftly from the States to Europe, hip hop was to dominate the 1980s as a leading subcultural movement.

Salt-N-Pepa epitomise flygirl style in 1987 with their heavy gold chains and tight catsuits.

To the flygirls and B-boys, as they were known, the sneaker was everything. Hip hop group Run-DMC paid homage to the trainer with their song 'My Adidas' in 1986. They wore their trainers unlaced, in the style of prisoners in jail, who had to hand their laces in to the authorities.

Initially the girls dressed like the boys, in loose tracksuits, **trainers**, caps and large gold jewellery. Later they cultivated their own look, embodied in the sartorial style of hip hop stars Salt-N-Pepa and Roxanne Shanté. They wore bomber jackets, tight leggings, oversized gold earrings and name belts – though tight bright jersey minidresses and **hot pants** were a sexier look for summer and stage. The trainers most in demand were by Adidas, Puma and Nike, with underwear by Calvin Klein. Some rappers, such as Queen Latifah, promoted Afrocentric clothing such as Africa-shaped pendants and clothes coloured the red, green and black of the Afro–American flag, and combined it with **sport**swear.

The designers were quick to catch on. In the late 1980s, Isaac Mizrahi designed a hip hop-inspired collection that included black catsuits and fur-trimmed black bomber jackets, with big gold chains and belts. Even Chanel gave a nod to hip hop style, dressing up black dresses with large padlocked silver chains, as worn by Treach of Naughty by Nature (the padlock jewellery was said to show respect for his friends in prison).

The hip hop fraternity coveted designer labels such as Gucci, Tommy Hilfiger and Chanel. When Snoop Doggy Dogg appeared on *Saturday Night Live* in 1994 wearing an oversized Hilfiger sweatshirt, sales rocketed in New York and the sweatshirt reputedly sold out. Female hip hop stars of the 1990s, such as Lil' Kim and Foxy Brown, promoted ultra-glamorous high fashion for the girls, and new labels including Baby Phat sprang up to meet the demand. After the 1990s a host of hip hop stars including Sean 'Puff Daddy' Combs, Nelly, Jay-Z, 50 Cent and others decided to cash in on their fashion following, and started up their own fashion labels to sell and promote their on-stage style. ∎

Rapper Treach from Naughty by Nature performs on the Tommy Hilfiger catwalk in 1996.

'A garment price tag on show even became a status symbol'

You are what you wear

IDEA № 85

BRAND CULTURE AND LOGO WORSHIP

Flaunting shop labels became a status symbol.

The 1980s ushered in a yuppie culture of work hard, play hard and sweat it all off at the gym afterwards. It was the decade of making it big – big hair, big breasts, big expense accounts, big jewellery and big shoulders. And it was fashionable to be seen to be splashing the cash.

It was also a decade of fashion companies using big marketing budgets and expensive ad campaigns to raise the profiles of their brands. They were selling the image rather than the actual product, and cashing in. And the consumer was led by the nose.

With this ostentatious style of dressing, it became fashionable to wear your preferred label on your wrist, your belt or your chest – be it the relatively discreet polo player of Ralph Lauren, Chanel's linked Cs or the designer logos of Versace, Moschino and Dior. For **sport**s and casualwear the essential logos were the Nike swoosh and the Adidas stripes. If you could not afford the head-to-toe look, you could say it with accessories – a Louis Vuitton bag, a Rolex watch, a Moschino belt or Chanel **sunglasses**. On the street, a price tag on show even became a status symbol.

Logos had been around for decades. Georges Vuitton branded early twentieth-century luggage with the Louis Vuitton initials and iconic flower. In the 1920s Jean Patou monogrammed knitwear, while Coco Chanel, Christian Dior, Pierre Cardin, Yves Saint Laurent and then Ralph Lauren and Calvin Klein were masters of brand-building. But in the 1980s it was vital to show your logo. Naomi Klein wrote in her book *No Logo* (2000): 'Gradually, the logo was transformed from an ostentatious affectation to an active fashion

accessory. Most significantly, the logo itself was growing in size, ballooning from a three-quarter-inch emblem into a chest-sized marquee.'

By the 1990s the big-budget marketing campaigns had backfired for some of the luxury brands. The ordinary person on the street started to wear clothing and accessories bearing the logos or insignia of such brands as Burberry, but teaming them with casual and high-street clothing. This damaged the brands' luxury image. Loud logos went out, and the marketing machines had to work even harder to validate and sell the new designer clothes that looked minimalist and utilitarian rather than obviously expensive.

Today the consumer has become more demanding, more savvy and less prone to brand loyalty. He or she wants something individual and of real value if it bears a high price tag – a limited edition handbag, or a one-off vintage piece. Clothing and accessories by successful fashion brands (but with subtle logos) are still sought after, but it is much more chic to own something that is rare or unavailable to others, or that only those in the know can recognize as elite and special. ■

Ex-soap star Daniella Westbrook overdoes the Burberry check on London's Bond Street, 2004.

From backpacks to bum bags

UTILITARIAN BAGS

When designer Miuccia Prada launched a black **nylon** rucksack with no logo in 1985, it provided a welcome antidote to the showy designer bags of that decade. Stark, minimal and fitted with plain leather straps, it was inspired by **sport**swear and military accessories. When Prada decided to add a logo, it was low-key – a simple flat triangular metal tag.

Brown rucksack with a beige leather trim by Louis Vuitton for Spring/Summer 2010.

The idea of luxury goods made from industrial materials appealed, and the backpack was soon the bag of choice for many urban women. It was no-nonsense and stylish and kept the hands free for public transport and shopping. Other brands copied fast, and the clean lines and simple practicality of these utilitarian bags became essentials for the girl about town. Gucci's backpack was in terracotta suede, while Donna Karan went for the Eurotrash look in buckled white, and a Louis Vuitton version was executed in the signature Vuitton monogram canvas.

Nineties clothes and accessories lent considerable emphasis to hands-free storage, with bags or pockets that hung outside garments. The 'J' bag was designed to be slung across the chest, with its single strap and asymmetric lines. Chanel produced bum bags in quilted fabric that hung from belts. There were messenger bags, belt bags, arm packs and body pouches by companies such as Yak Pak.

Instead of leather, designers opted for modern fabrics such as nylon and polyester with sportswear-inspired waterproof coatings. Backpacks became flatter, sitting closer to the body like another layer of clothing. In line with the fashionable parkas and combat trousers, military-inspired bag design,

such as holster bags, became popular on the street. A flat white Helmut Lang body bag was to be worn strapped around the waist and attached to the thigh like a large removable pocket. In pursuing pure practicality above all else, these bags openly rejected any notions of elegance. Strapped uncompromisingly to the back or the waist, they presented a silhouette that was anything but feminine. ∎

The bumbag, a 1980s favourite, comes back into fashion for 2010.

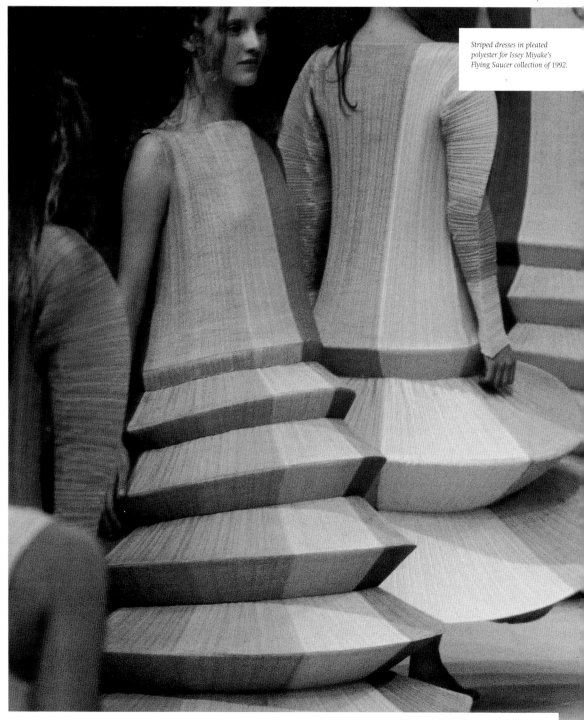

Striped dresses in pleated polyester for Issey Miyake's Flying Saucer collection of 1992.

'The designers helped to redefine the preconceived ideals of the female silhouette'

Fabric drives fashion

IDEA № 87

JAPANESE DESIGN

When the Japanese designers came to Paris in the 1980s, they tossed all Western preconceptions and assumptions about fashion up into the air, introducing their own materials, ideas and cuts. They were to make waves that rocked the fashion world with their new aesthetic.

Issey Miyake shows a directional design in black in Paris for Spring/Summer 1994.

Kenzo Takada and Kansai Yamamoto were already showing in Paris by the 1980s. Yohji Yamamoto and Issey Miyake joined them, along with Rei Kawakubo and her label Comme des Garçons.

Miyake played with new fibres and garment construction in a way that had never been seen before in the West: tunics and stoles of pleated synthetic and metallic yarn; hats created from polyurethane foam sheeting; wind coats more reminiscent of parachutes than clothing; moulded body corsets of the female torso. His pieces often hung away from the body rather than following its natural curves.

Kawakubo of Comme des Garçons perfected the idea of conceptual fashion, deconstructing garments to remake them into something new and surprising. She introduced holes into knitwear and in 1996 produced a series of bizarre dresses swollen with padded fabric like unconstrained areas of bulging flesh. Together with Yohji Yamamoto, Kawakubo also helped to inspire the all-black urban uniform seen today on so many city streets.

Yamamoto was one of the founding fathers of minimalism, and a master of the cut. Rather than fitting a piece of clothing to the body with conventional seams, he used layering and volume to make garments that wrapped the figure loosely. This way of dressing was new to Western eyes, and explained by Issey Miyake: 'The cut of a Western garment is determined by the body, a Japanese one by the fabric.'

Between them, the designers helped to redefine the preconceived ideals of the female silhouette, with garments that would impose their own rules on the body. But it took a confident woman to sacrifice showing off her carefully honed curves for this subtler Japanese style of dress. ∎

The new urban uniform

IDEA № 88

STREETWEAR

In fashion, 'streetwear' means more than literally what people are wearing on the street. It refers to an urban youth movement and mode of dress, which started in 1980s New York. Street style involved elements of Californian skateboard and surf culture, **hip hop**, **punk** and Rastafarian clothing: the look was urban, **sport**y and practical.

A Stussy advertisement from the 1980s, selling loose, easy streetwear with influences from the Californian surf scene.

Engle hooded shirt with a country check by Staple Design for Spring/Summer 2010.

When the white New York band the Beastie Boys exploded onto the scene in 1986 with their punk-inspired hip hop album *Licensed to Ill*, they personified this urban street look with their **trainers**, hooded tops and branded T-shirts. They took Volkswagen insignia ripped from cars and hung them from chains around their necks: naturally their fans copied them, much to the fury of unsuspecting VW owners.

Streetwear could not be divided into daywear and evening wear – the same loose trousers, trainers, big T-shirts and casual jackets could be worn on the street during the day or in a club at night. Streetwear changed fashion. It created an urban uniform that spread beyond the United States to Japan and Europe, and spawned a host of new clothing brands during the 1980s and 1990s, such as SSUR, New York's Staple Design and ONETrueSaxon.

The timing was perfect. Designer fashion from Paris had started to be regarded as stuffy and overpriced by some urban youth, and this made way for the cooler street brands that offered dressed-down clothes. It looked hipper and more youthful, cost less and had a tantalizingly underground feel. It appealed to those who felt their lifestyles were far removed from catwalk shows and luxury designer boutiques, but who could respect urban brands that were started as small businesses (often initially as T-shirt collections) by people like them – with similar interests in music, art or sport scenes such as punk, hip hop, graffiti, surfing and snowboarding.

Erik Brunetti started his label FUCT in the 1990s after working as a graffiti artist and designing skateboard artwork. Hiroshi Fujiwara, regarded as one of the most influential streetwear designers, worked as a DJ and music producer and was influenced by punk culture. The designers of US label X Large were architects. One of the most respected streetwear pioneers was Shawn Stussy, a surfer in California. He started to print T-shirts bearing his name, in the style of a graffiti tag, during the 1980s surf boom and sold them alongside surfboards. Today Stussy is a hugely successful urban street-style brand, mixing influences from skatewear, workwear and army surplus. The streetwear legacy lives on. ∎

Streetwear aficionados
Beastie Boys strike a pose
at Capitol Records in 1992.

'It appealed to those who felt their lifestyles
were far removed from catwalk shows'

A London clubber on the new rave scene celebrates the origins of the movement with the Smiley face insignia and clashing bright coloured accessories, 2007.

'The energetic party animals who went to raves wore coloured loose jeans and hooded tops with trainers and bright hats'

The power of Smiley culture

IDEA № 89

RAVE

The rave scene emerged in Britain and America during the 1980s, centred around electronic dance music such as acid house and techno, and creating its own fashion and culture. Unusually, it brought together young people from very different backgrounds, united by an appetite for the music, parties and, often, drugs, particularly Ecstasy.

House and acid house music had developed as part of the 1980s Chicago club scene in America, when DJs began to make music using electronic synthesizer-sequencers. It spread to other cities such as New York and Detroit, and then to Australia and Europe, particularly the UK. There, the movement took off after a group of London DJs was influenced by the combination of early house music and the drug Ecstasy in the open-air clubs of Ibiza in the summer of 1985. On their return, they opened clubs such as Shoom and Project Club in London to continue the Ibiza vibe, while in Manchester, the Hacienda Club started to introduce nights playing acid house music.

As the movement spread in the UK, more clubs opened, and illegal parties started to be held in warehouses. During the late 1980s and early 1990s, illegal raves held in office blocks, aircraft hangars, clubs, car parks or simply open fields attracted thousands of young ravers, who took Ecstasy and danced to music with fast repetitive beats. Venues were often kept secret until the evening of the party, when ravers had to call a special phone number to discover the location. The huge raves, often lasting all weekend, were similar to the festivals of the 1960s, though with less free love and more dancing; 1988 was dubbed the Second Summer of Love.

The energetic party animals who went to raves wore coloured loose **jeans** and hooded tops, accessorized with **trainers** and bright hats – and an obligatory whistle for the dancefloor. T-shirts and tops were emblazoned with psychedelic prints and patterns. The emblem of the movement became the yellow Smiley face, which appeared on T-shirts, badges and pendants. As New Age travellers joined forces with the ravers to organize festivals and parties, dreadlocks, piercings and combat trousers worn with bright T-shirts became part of the traveller–raver uniform.

In 1994 the Criminal Justice and Public Order Bill clamped down on unlicensed outdoor music events, and the rave spirit and culture in the UK dwindled. But rave fashion re-emerged in 2006 as new rave, with bright, fluorescent, **sports**-inspired **streetwear** covered in Smiley face emblems, and catwalk versions of the look designed by Gareth Pugh, Christopher Kane and Karen Walker. ∎

TOP: *Dancing in a field at the Glastonbury Festival in the UK, 1995, in a toned-down New Age take on rave clothing.*

ABOVE: *A smiling raver dances at the club Shoom in London, 1988.*

Shock tactics to sell clothes

IDEA № 90

THE BENETTON ADVERTISING CAMPAIGNS

A nun kisses a priest. A white baby suckles at a black breast. A blood-streaked newborn baby takes its first breath, its umbilical cord still attached. These are some of the controversial and award-winning advertising images that creative director Oliviero Toscani masterminded for the clothing brand Benetton between 1982 and 2000.

Toscani created this Benetton advertisement to coincide with the 1992 Olympic Games in Barcelona.

Toscani was a master of publicity, and he succeeded in selling clothes for Benetton through controversy. In 1984 he photographed groups of models of all races wearing Benetton clothing, for the 'All the Colors of the World' advertisements. It was daring for the time. After 1989, his more political and shocking images started to appear on billboards and in magazines, with no images of the clothes at all. His ads resembled pieces of fine art – a famous campaign included a photograph of a man dying of AIDS, which caused controversy mainly thanks to its resemblance to a *Pietà* painting – but the company used them very successfully to sell clothes.

Toscani changed the ideas behind fashion advertising, proving that images devoid of fashion references and imagery could still be used to sell. It was a clever move, as consumers of all races, worldwide, could interpret in their own way the photographs that drew on the big themes of human experience – life, death, war and religion.

In 2000 Toscani pushed the limits of taste too far with a Benetton campaign entitled 'We, on Death Row', which showed portraits of condemned men, convicted killers. There was a public outcry. 'Benetton is glamorizing killers,' said a member of the victims of crime group Justice for All. 'Benetton has built their campaign on the blood of victims.' When the retailer Sears, Roebuck and Co. axed its Benetton clothing franchise, Benetton and Toscani finally parted company. 'If the death sentence were handed out to those who are guilty of producing excruciatingly tasteless, ineffective advertising and inflicting it on the masses, Oliviero Toscani, the self-proclaimed genius behind Benetton advertising, would be appearing in his own anti-capital-punishment ads,' raged Jerry Della Femina in the *Wall Street Journal*.

Toscani's novel approach of excluding the very clothing that he was advertising, twinned with unforgettable images, meant that his work dramatically raised the profile of a brand that had been known until then principally for its brightly coloured jumpers. He not only built his career, he helped to rebuild the Benetton brand. ∎

UNITED COLORS OF BENETTON.

Toscani's controversial 1991 advertisement for Benetton featuring a newborn baby is arrestingly raw and dramatic.

New downbeat Belgian design

Innovative Belgian designer Martin Margiela shows loose layered outsize garments, with hair to match, in 2000. The uneven raw cuffs are typical of his signature style.

IDEA № 91

DECONSTRUCTION AND ANTWERP

In the 1980s, six avant-garde designers who had trained at the Royal Academy of Fine Arts in Antwerp, Belgium, decided to launch their talents in London. They included Ann Demeulemeester, Dries Van Noten and Dirk Bikkembergs. With Martin Margiela, who launched his first Paris collection in 1989, they introduced a radical low-key style of dress for the 1990s.

Although each had his or her own individual style, they often worked with distressed clothes in monotone colours. Martin Margiela and Ann Demeulemeester enjoyed reassembling clothes, and introduced tailoring with unstitched seams, exposed lining and frayed edges. They steered away from colour, and focused on detail and contrasting fabrics. Margiela incorporated antique tulle and patchwork from flea markets into his work, and put seams and zips on the outside of garments. The press labelled it Deconstruction, although he disagreed with the term. 'I don't see the idea of "deconstruction",' he said. 'When I slash down old or new clothes to transform them I do not believe that I am destroying them, but bringing them back to life in a different way.' Margiela went on to design for Hermès in 1997.

Demeulemeester focused on layered, flowing clothes, without ostentatious colour, instead using texture as ornamentation. She became known for her long coats and dresses, as well as trousers cut radically low to show off the hip bone; she also put laddered stockings on the catwalk.

Dries Van Noten's work was more feminine. Referencing the East, he layered sarongs, jackets and trousers, using dark colours and minimal ornamentation.

Dirk Bikkembergs started out as a menswear designer, launching womenswear in 1993. He focussed on offering minimalist, strong shapes in muted tones that he then treated with his deconstructed aesthetic. He is well known for using, and often layering, wool and leather, and for his strong military influences.

Their timing was perfect, with a downbeat look that would not have worked during the showy 1980s, but instead fed the next decade's modest appetite for minimal ostentation and clothes that looked more authentic and unfinished. ∎

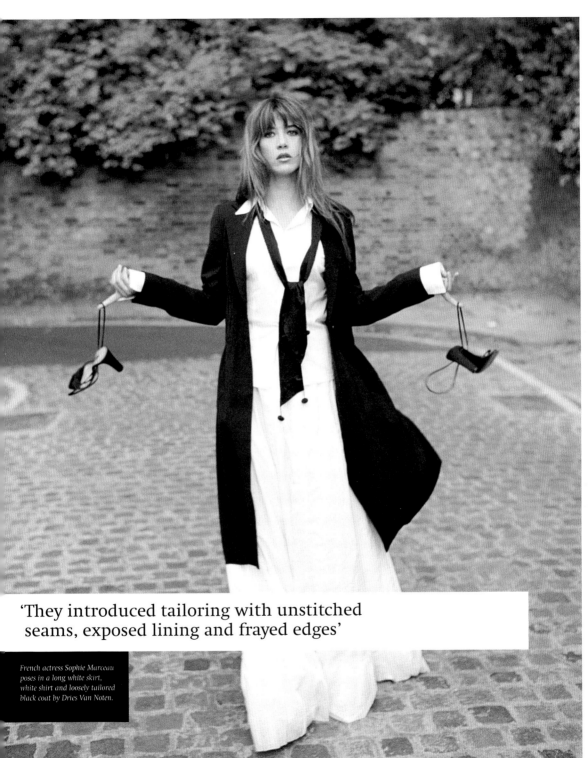

'They introduced tailoring with unstitched seams, exposed lining and frayed edges'

French actress Sophie Marceau poses in a long white skirt, white shirt and loosely tailored black coat by Dries Van Noten.

'Some designers choose to host their fashion shows on the Internet, streaming images directly into domestic computer screens'

CLOCKWISE FROM TOP: *Pages from luxury online shopping site net-a-porter; the official website of designer John Galliano; cult fashion blog The Sartorialist.*

Fashion in cyberspace

THE INTERNET

Developed initially by the US military during the Cold War as a response to the Soviet launch of Sputnik in 1957, with the intention of regaining the technological upper hand, the Internet began life as ARPANET. It developed progressively throughout the 1960s, '70s and '80s to become a globe-encompassing network.

It was still mainly used by the military and academics, however, and it was not until Tim Berners-Lee invented the World Wide Web in the late 1980s that public use took off.

The Internet has had a dramatic impact on many aspects of modern life, including the fashion industry. In order to hold their own in the market, all leading brands today have their own promotional websites, showing the latest collections, press office information and links to their stores and stockists. Designers were quick to latch on to the marketing potential of websites, and the Internet has become a valuable research tool for members of the public seeking brand and stockist information.

Catwalk shows and new street trends are transmitted straight to consumers' homes as they happen, with a startling immediacy that has never before been possible. Websites such as style.com and firstview.com became some of the first to publish photographs and videos from the international fashion weeks. Some designers choose to host their fashion shows on the Internet rather than as live events,

streaming images directly into domestic computer screens. Burberry launched a click-and-buy formula, through which customers can order selected items online while watching its catwalk show – and the pieces will be delivered just seven weeks later. 'The fast pace dictated by the Internet is rewriting the archaic rules of the fashion industry. Live streaming of catwalk shows and the rise of a generation of bloggers have formed a direct connection between catwalk and customer,' wrote Jess Cartner-Morley in the *Guardian* in 2010.

Retail has been revolutionized, with thousands of online shopping sites selling everything from vintage designer-wear to new labels. Jackets and shoes can be ordered and delivered to the home with just a few clicks of the mouse, with the innumerable online retailers ranging from high-street multiples to high-end luxury retailers such as net-a-porter.com. New designers can now sell directly to consumers through the Internet, without any need of an intermediary.

Magazines and newspapers, long at the heart of the industry, have been

quick to adapt and join the online world. Every leading magazine now publishes its online version and some have abandoned the print product altogether. Consumers, who now expect live news coverage, continue to shun traditional printed newspapers for the online alternatives.

A torrent of new competition from blogs, Internet magazines and the social media commentary on Facebook, Instagram, Twitter and Snapchat is reshaping the industry. Fashion coverage on YouTube and Instagram by fashion influencers and big-name bloggers has made the brands sit up and collaborate with them. The fact that anyone can self-publish online has helped to democratize fashion and the old guard has had to run with the changes, or risk being left behind.

The Internet has had a positive effect on fashion for the consumer, empowering them but also making them more demanding. Information and increasing choice means that retailers, brands and the media have to work harder to please an ever more impatient fashion-savvy public. ∎

'It was time to take stock and re-evaluate after the extravagant fashion of the 1980s'

The New Age look was cool, calm and simple, and executed in pure white.

The dawn of a bright, white future

THE NEW PURITY

In 1990 the London-based Turkish designer Rifat Ozbek captivated critics and buyers with his all-white New Age collection, a refreshing series of loose separates influenced by clubbing, **sport** and **streetwear**. Ozbek reworked tracksuits and sports clothing into cool, comfortable clubwear, including sequined baseball caps, loose white hooded tops and pieces bearing slogans such as 'Nirvana'.

It was a fresh chapter in fashion, as had been Courrèges' **Space Age** collection in the 1960s. The Gulf War had shut off the lucrative markets of the Arab world, so it was a sobering time for the fashion houses. Ecological concerns were on people's minds. It was time to take stock and re-evaluate after the decorative consumption and extravagant fashion of the 1980s, with its often brash opulence. Ozbek's collection played to a clean, rehabilitative and calm spiritual mood. A less-is-more approach to fashion was to become one of the most important elements that defined 1990s style, particularly as it was so different from that of the previous decade. *i-D* magazine reported: 'In 1993, fashion has subjected itself to a reality check. Excessive flamboyance is now seen as a touch distasteful. Interest has shifted towards a movement that rejects gloss in favour of an acceptance of the political and economic turmoil of the times.'

Fashion saw a return to simple luxury separates, led by such designers as the American Zoran, who created capsule wardrobes in fine fabrics. Zoran concentrated on simplicity, perfecting the loose pyjama trouser and T-shirt, and kept accessories and fastenings to a minimum.

Throughout the final decade of the twentieth century, fashion quietened down its tone. Designers concentrated on sleek clothes, which were subtle, comfortable and, above all else, unshowy. ■

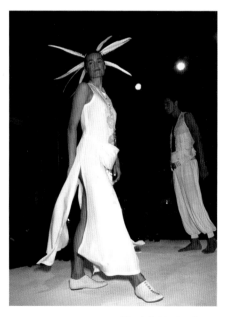

Relaxed all-white pieces from the iconic 1990 New Age collection by Rifat Ozbek.

*Muji T-shirts are pointedly
unbranded, and Muji prides
itself on its lack of aggressive
marketing.*

Just say no to the logo

THE ANTI-BRAND

How can a brand be unbranded? What, indeed, is an anti-brand? The 1990s saw the emergence of new companies whose philosophy was a reaction to the excesses of the 1980s. They began to build their names on the back of anti-consumerist ideals.

There was generally a new, moderating attitude to consumption in the 1990s, caused by an ailing worldwide economy. Fashion designers focused on **low-key luxury**, and bold logos came to be seen as vulgar.

In 2000 Naomi Klein published the influential book *No Logo*, chronicling the way in which brands had become more important than the products themselves, and taking a hard, critical look at the power of multinational corporations and our obsession with branding and consumption. Klein caught the mood of the time, and the anti-branding, anti-globalization movement went on to grow, with many fashion companies embracing its ideals. This paradoxically allowed them to build brands in a new way, but also encouraged them to take responsibility for their sourcing and manufacturing policies.

Today anti-branding is gaining momentum. The advent of **the Internet** has required companies to show more transparency, and those that are unethical or greedy risk becoming targets of global slur campaigns, which can be costly and damaging.

The Japanese company Muji went multinational in the late 1980s, offering simply designed clothing and interiors products. Muji prided itself on its lack of aggressive marketing and branding. A statement on the Muji website read: 'MUJI is not a brand. MUJI does not make products of individuality or fashion.' It launched a T-shirt with a blank space for the wearer to create his or her own logo.

In 2004 Adidas opened an unbranded store in London simply called 6 Newburgh Street. This no-nonsense approach aimed to convey authenticity to the consumer, in stark contrast to its heavily branded rivals.

Similarly, the multiple retailer American Apparel, selling mainly basic though fashion-led T-shirts and dresses in cotton jersey, vaunted its non-branded clothing and individually designed stores. The first shops opened in Canada and North America in 2003. All the clothing was made in the United States, and never in sweatshops abroad. The company used anti-corporate and anti-globalization ideas to market its products. Its advertising campaigns, featuring non-professional models, were carefully calculated to appeal to a new breed of questioning young shoppers.

Some argue that these anti-brand companies are merely using new marketing techniques to achieve the same goals as those corporations they profess to despise. Nonetheless, they tap into a desire on the part of those modern consumers who are increasingly asking questions about the products they buy, and demanding responsibility from their suppliers and manufacturers. And this consciousness has to be a positive thing. ∎

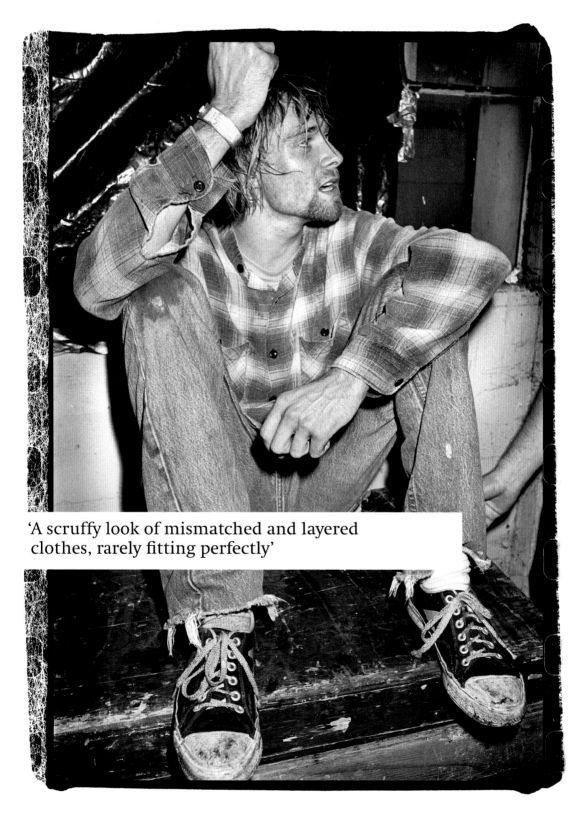

'A scruffy look of mismatched and layered clothes, rarely fitting perfectly'

High fashion dresses down

ABOVE: *The influential Perry Ellis Spring/Summer 1993 grunge show, designed by Marc Jacobs.*

OPPOSITE: *Grunge rock icon Kurt Cobain of Nirvana in Seattle, 1990.*

IDEA Nº 95

GRUNGE

Take a **punk** and a hippie, chew them up, roll them around your mouth and then spit them out. You have created grunge. Although a relatively small subcultural movement, grunge had an impact on fashion that was far larger than its original following. It tapped into the downbeat mood of the 1990s and into consumers' needs to buy into something 'real', a world away from the logo- and status-obsessed 1980s.

Grunge evolved in Seattle, a subgenre of American rock made famous by such bands as Pearl Jam and Nirvana. The word 'grunge' originated in the 1960s, when grungy meant dirty. Like the music it accompanied, grunge style was essentially anti-fashion, and about dressing down: a scruffy look of mismatched and layered clothes, usually oversized or undersized – rarely fitting perfectly. Kurt Cobain, the lead singer of Nirvana, epitomized the grunge look with his dishevelled hair, **jeans**, checked shirt and Converse shoes. The girls favoured short floral dresses teamed with heavy army boots, also pairing big jumpers with crumpled silk tops.

Grunge started on the street, but was quickly seized by such designers as Anna Sui, who incorporated the look into her catwalk collection for Spring/Summer 1993. In 1992 Marc Jacobs had presented a grunge-inspired collection for Perry Ellis of skull caps, work boots, flannel shirts and silk dresses worn with cashmere thermals. *The New York Times* described it as 'a mess', and it was, perhaps unsurprisingly, Jacobs' last collection for Perry Ellis. More unpredictably, grunge was also interpreted by designers Christian Lacroix, Donna Karan for DKNY, Ralph Lauren, and Karl Lagerfeld for Chanel. However, designer ready-to-wear clients were reluctant to pay high prices for street-style clothes. It was not the 1980s, but they still wanted a little bit of luxury for their money. So grunge swiftly returned to the street – back where it belonged. ∎

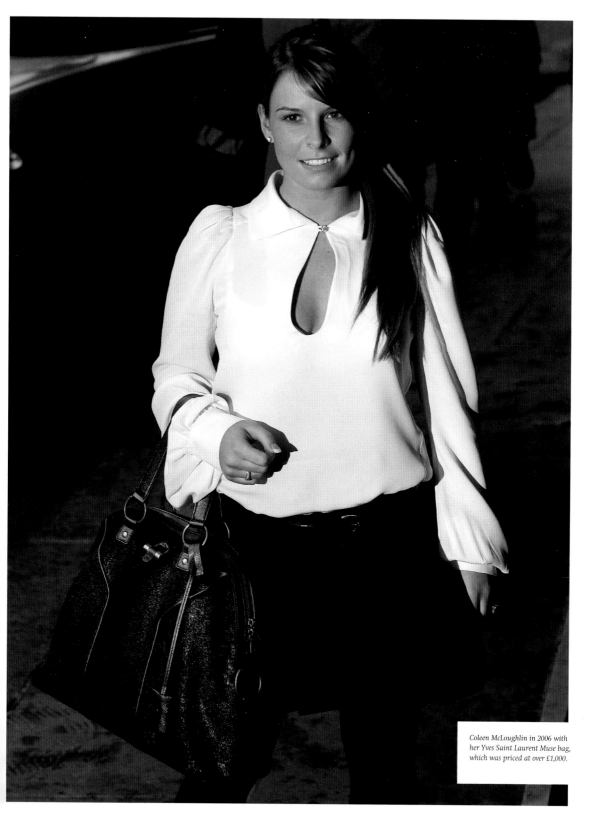

Coleen McLoughlin in 2006 with her Yves Saint Laurent Muse bag, which was priced at over £1,000.

Waiting lists and four-figure price tags

Grace Kelly announces her engagement to Prince Rainier of Monaco in 1956, carrying an Hermès bag. It was later named the Kelly Bag in her honour.

IDEA № 96

THE STATUS HANDBAG

Status handbags are some of today's most conspicuous marks of wealth and consumption, with prices running to many thousands of pounds. A desirable designer bag often has a long waiting list of well-heeled customers anxious to buy it and flaunt their ownership.

Women's handbags in the 1980s were often made from newer and more economical materials than leather, and women got into the habit of combining different handbags with their various outfits.

By the 1990s clothing had become fashionably low-key (some might say boring) and canny designers realized that glamorous women wearing understated clothes would pay a great deal to acquire the perfect accessory by a luxury brand. By making only limited runs of their signature bags, they could generate enormous demand and long waiting lists.

The designer labels Prada, Dior, Fendi and Gucci commanded astronomical sums for their much sought-after handbags. Designer Marc Jacobs joined Louis Vuitton in 1997 and his injection of inspiration saw the company's sales of leather goods grow by nearly a third. The designers at Fendi scored particularly well with their Baguette bag, which tucks under the arm like a French loaf – a reputed 600,000 were sold in just three years, and it is still going strong. The Christian Dior Saddle bag, the Yves Saint Laurent Muse and the Chloé Paddington sent women running for their Amex cards.

By 2005 handbags were the best-selling items of women's fashion merchandise. This goldmine enticed companies without handbag lines, such as designers Narciso Rodriguez and Zac Posen, to rush in and launch their own accessories collections.

The major design houses continued to employ their classic bag shapes, but revived them with different materials and finishes from season to season. The more exotic finishes accounted for the five-figure price tags of some bags. Hermès continues to this day to sell the Kelly Bag, named after Grace Kelly and first launched in the 1950s, updating it in different finishes and materials. Karl Lagerfeld also updates the distinctive long-chained 2.55 bag for Chanel each year.

One of the hottest and most exclusive status bags is the Birkin, made by Hermès and named after the 1960s actress Jane Birkin. Both Martha Stewart and rapper Lil' Kim carried one for their court hearings. There is a two-year waiting list to buy them and they cost over $5,000. It is certainly a quiet way of making a bold statement in court. ∎

Textiles get clever

PERFORMANCE FABRICS

Fabrics and fibres can perform, as well as look fashionable – keep the wearer dry, protect from harmful bacteria or against UV rays, or even dose the body with vitamin C or moisturizer.

This revolutionary Prada raincoat from Autumn/Winter 2002 turns opaque in the rain.

Performance fabrics are synthetic technical fabrics that have been developed with a specific functional purpose in mind, often for the **sport**s, military or medical industries. But it is not all about antibacterial or flame-retardant textiles: fashion designers have been quick to seize on some of the new fabrics for their collections. Versace and Issey Miyake were at the forefront of fabric technology during the 1980s, and by the 1990s designers were intrigued by the new ideas on offer from the major textile houses and textile fairs.

The fashion industry made full use of the new fabric technology, using some of its protective qualities in clothing. Junya Watanabe used a waterproof fabric that, rather than being coated to keep the rain out, trapped air and pushed water droplets to the surface. For his ski and cycle collections Ralph Lauren used Gore-Tex, which is breathable, windproof and waterproof. In sun-scorched Australia, Coolibar launched a range of clothing that blocked more than 97 percent of the sun's rays. Similarly, Evoluzione garments in treated cotton boasted a sun-protection factor of 40 and a promise to keep the body between five and ten degrees cooler. Dockers incorporated lined pockets in its trousers, which, it claimed, would shield users from mobile phone radiation. An extraordinary 2002 Prada innovation was a sheer raincoat that turned opaque in the rain.

To help stave off winter colds, Fuji Spinning Co. in Japan came up with a T-shirt in 2001 that doses the wearer with vitamin C on contact with warm human skin. The company Cherie launched **tights** that moisturize the legs with aloe vera.

Fragrance has been popular in lingerie ranges. La Perla made sweet-smelling underwear by embedding particles of fragrance into the fabric. More extreme was Triumph's prototype anti-smoking bra, whose aromatherapy odours of jasmine and lavender were intended to stop the craving for nicotine.

For sportswear and underwear, the high-tech Coolmax fibre draws sweat away from the body towards a garment's surface, so the body can breathe and air will circulate.

Scientists have produced exciting new textiles as a result of Nanotechnology – working with materials at a tiny scale. After years of research into self-healing textiles, garments such as the 2017 Nano Cure Tech jacket by Imperial Motion made it into the mainstream. In order to repair a tear, rub the fabric with your fingers and the heat of your skin bonds it back together. Even better are clothes that don't need to be washed. By 2016 a team of scientists from RMIT University in Melbourne had developed a Nano-enhanced self-cleaning textile that only needs a dose of sunlight or artificial light to keep clean. The domestic dream was slowly becoming a reality. Goodbye washing machines, hello clean clothes – and lots more free time. ∎

'Triumph's prototype anti-smoking
bra was intended to stop the craving
for nicotine'

ABOVE AND RIGHT: *Sportswear by Adidas.*

Like mother, like daughter

IDEA № 98
ETERNAL YOUTH

By the end of the twentieth century, it was quite acceptable for three generations of women to wear the same style of clothing. Dress no longer had to be determined by the wearer's age, and a 70-year-old could shop at the same stores as her 18-year-old granddaughter.

Siblings? No. Actress Demi Moore and her daughter Tallulah Belle Willis in 2007.

Women of all ages were highly fashion-aware at the end of the 1990s. Healthy diet and exercise, an increasing rejection of smoking, and great advances in medicine had all led to women living longer. And also to looking younger: tremendous efforts were made to avoid looking old.

Cosmetics were continually being updated with new technology, and the creeping acceptance of cosmetic surgery allowed women, for a price, to retain their youthful good looks. With Botox treatment becoming widely available, it was goodbye to wrinkles and hello to smooth foreheads. Hair, eyelash and nail extensions and fake tan were marketed to cater to the illusion of eternal perfectibility.

Conversely, while the old sought to perpetuate their youth, the young increasingly aspired to dress like adults. Children's fashion ranges have encouraged the young to emulate adult trends, and precocious girls to mimic their pop icons. If children were not always treated like adults, they could at least dress like them. Today's pubescent girls are also physically and socially much more advanced than their early-twentieth-century counterparts. While the average age for the onset of menstruation in Victorian times was 16, it is today a mere 11.

The practice of children dressing as adults has a long and respectable history. Medieval and Renaissance portraits show small children dressed in all the extravagance of grown-up fashion. These often included 'ruffs, padded breeches, trailing sleeves, dragging skirts, high-heeled shoes and hats top-heavy with feathers and flowers', as Alison Lurie noted in *The Language of Clothes* (1981). It was not until the late eighteenth century that children were encouraged to wear loose fashions of their own that allowed them to run and play, instead of being dressed as small adults straight after infancy.

Life expectancy continues to grow in the West. With today's new babies expected to live beyond the age of 100, can it be long before the same fashions appeal across five generations? ∎

Dress no longer indicates age. Jade Jagger poses with her daughters Amba, 12, and Assisi, 15, in 2008.

'Hair, eyelash and nail extensions and fake tan were marketed to cater to the illusion of eternal perfectibility'

Fashion's green credentials

Eco campaigner and designer Katharine Hamnett on an Oxfam-sponsored visit to highlight the plight of cotton farmers in Mali, 2003.

IDEA № 99

SUSTAINABLE FASHION

The 1990s was a decade of great change, not least in consumers' awareness of climate change and other, interrelated environmental issues such as pesticide use, pollution and waste. As global warming became a more widely accepted challenge, so the fashion world started to respond with eco-friendly clothing and eco fashion.

Although the **hippies** embraced notions of sustainability as early as the 1960s, their impact on mainstream fashion was slight. 'Nobody wanted to know about fashion and ethics 20 years ago,' said Katharine Hamnett in 2008. Hamnett led the way, using environmentally friendly fabrics such as organic cotton, and eventually fair-trade and ecological fashion brands became more common. People Tree, for example, which was set up in 1997, worked with organic producers in developing countries, and sold fair-trade and organic clothing.

Second-hand clothing became known as vintage, and was suddenly chic. Expensive vintage stores opened up to cater for the demand. In 1992 Helen Storey started a high-fashion recycled label, entitled Second Life.

During the late 1990s the fashion and clothing manufacturing industries began to respond to fair-trade issues. Brands such as Nike and Sean John were exposed in the media for alleged bad practice, and many sweatshops in developing countries were shut down. Eco fashion became big business with increasing interest in fabric made from organic natural fibres, such as hemp, cotton, silk and linen. Slowly, high-end designers including Diane von Furstenberg and Proenza Schouler started to do their bit. Stella McCartney became a pioneer of promoting sustainability in fashion claiming: 'We are agents of change. We challenge and push boundaries to make luxurious products in a way that is fit for the world we live in today and the future: beautiful and sustainable. No compromises.'

By the 2010s Biotechnology – using living systems and organisms such as bacteria and algae to develop products – had become a fashion buzzword. Suzanne Lee, at BioCouture started growing textiles made from living organisms and by 2018 Stella McCartney was developing a new biomaterial grown from mycelium, the underground root structure of fungi.

However, in spite of all these exciting developments on the surface, the fashion and textile industry continues to be one of the world's largest polluters, with a terrible track record for greenhouse gas emissions and landfill. Much, much more needs to be done. ∎

Recycled pleated polyester dress, hand-painted and beaded over a floral print, by Central Saint Martins (London, UK) graduate Davina Hawthorne, Spring/Summer 2008.

'Electrical and fabric engineers have started to embed electronics directly into textiles'

A dress with LED devices installed inside, designed by Swarovski and Hussein Chalayan, Tokyo, 2007.

The future is now

A Pioneer Corp employee shows the latest prototype in Japanese streetwear in 2002 – a hybrid of fashion and technology inspired by wearable PCs. The heatproof fabric display is embedded in the sleeve.

IDEA Nº 100

WEARABLE TECHNOLOGY

Computers and smart phones embedded into clothing is no longer a dream of the future. Wearable technology is changing the way we communicate and use clothing. Activity tracking bands and Apple watches are commonplace, and some predict that we will come to rely on a favourite jacket, as we do a mobile phone, as an essential communication tool.

In 1922 Alfred Dunhill installed a light in its handbags, which switched on when the bag was opened. A little later, Elsa Schiaparelli designed handbags that played music. But recent technological changes have been far more ambitious.

In 1999 the electronics company Philips collaborated with Levi Strauss on the ICD+ jacket. A mobile phone and an MP3 player sat in its pockets and connected to earphones via wires running through an integral hood, allowing you to switch between listening to music and taking a call. C'N'C Costume National developed bags with small solar panel strips for recharging an MP3 or mobile. However, electronics in garments looked clunky – and there was a big technical problem: they had to be removed before washing.

One solution was to use accessories rather than clothes. Hearing aids are an early example of wearable technology, but in the 2010s fitness bands were introduced, and then smartwatches. Samsung launched their Samsung Galaxy Gear smartwatch in 2013, and Apple followed in 2015 with its Apple Watch. Fitbit's activity-tracking wristband first came onto the market in 2009. GPS tracking shoes were even touted as an essential bit of safety kit by carers of dementia patients. However, this was just the beginning.

Motorcyclists have long been grateful for their battery-heated jackets and gloves. In the 2000s electrical and fabric engineers began to embed electronics directly into textiles, creating washable and stretchable electronic circuits. In 2002 Softswitch and Burton Snowboards launched one of the first commercial electronic garments – a snowboarding jacket with an integrated fabric control pad on the jacket sleeve linked to a mini-disc player. In 2008 O'Neill introduced the NavJacket, a ski jacket with built-in GPS on the sleeve.

Taking technology in a more fashion-driven direction, CuteCircuit produced a skirt whose colour and pattern could be changed by touch, and Hussein Chalayan played with clothes whose form and structure changed by remote control. Dutch designer Iris van Herpen incorporates 3D printing into her collections. She fuses traditional craft with technology, and works with sound and touch in fabric.

As technology advances ever faster and communications become more portable, it seems inevitable that the clothes we wear will become increasingly responsive and sophisticated. ∎

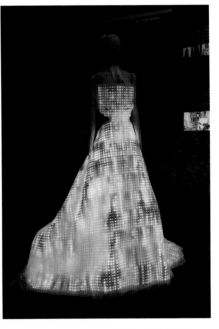

This lightweight silk Galaxy Dress by CuteCircuit from 2009 is embroidered with 24,000 paper-thin LEDs, and interspersed with over 4,000 hand-applied Swarovski crystals.

Further Reading

Books

David Bailey and Martin Harrison, *David Bailey: Archive One 1957–1969*, 1999

Hamish Bowles, *Yves Saint Laurent: Style*, 2008

Mariuccia Casadio, *Missoni (Made in Italy)*, 1998

Clifton Daniel, *20th Century Day by Day (DK Millennium)*, 1999

Christian Dior, *Dior by Dior*, 2007

Mick Farren, *The Black Leather Jacket*, 2008

Salvatore Ferragamo, *Shoemaker of Dreams: the autobiography of Salvatore Ferragamo*, 1972

Patty Fox, *Star Style: Hollywood Legends as Fashion Icons*, 1995

Neal Heard, *Trainers: Over 300 Classics, from Rare Vintage to the Latest Designs*, 2005

Tim Jackson and David Shaw, *The Fashion Handbook*, 2006

Naomi Klein, *No Logo*, 2000

Victor Margueritte, *La Garçonne*, 1922

Richard Martin, *Fashion and Surrealism*, 1989

Colin McDowell, *Galliano: Romantic, Realist and Revolutionary*, 1998

Patricia Mears and Steven Bluttal, *Halston*, 2001

PYMCA, Ted Polhemus, Jon Swinstead, and James Lange, *Unordinary People: British Youth Culture 1960–2009*, 2009

Ligaya Salazar, *Fashion V Sport*, 2008

Elsa Schiaparelli, *Shocking Life: The Autobiography of Elsa Schiaparelli*, 2007

Vivian Vale and Andrea Juno, *Modern Primitives: Investigation of Contemporary Adornment Rituals*, 1997

Louis Vuitton and Marc Jacobs, *Louis Vuitton: Art, Fashion and Architecture*, 2009

Claire Wilcox, *The Golden Age of Couture: Paris and London 1947–1957*, 2008

Anna Wintour and André Leon Talley, *Manolo Blahník Drawings*, 2003

Harriet Worsley, *Classics of Fashion*, 2002

Harriet Worsley, *Decades of Fashion*, 2006

Harriet Worsley, *The White Dress: Fashion Inspiration for Brides*, 2009

Films

American Gigolo, directed by Paul Schrader, 1980. (The shoulder pad)

Blow Up, directed by Michelangelo Antonioni, 1966. (Raw photography)

Clash By Night, directed by Fritz Lang, 1952. (Jeans)

Coco Before Chanel, directed by Anne Fontaine, 2009. (Trousers for women)

Desperately Seeking Susan, directed by Susan Seidelman, 1985. (Pop stars)

The Devil Wears Prada, directed by David Frankel, 2006. (Vogue)

Dishonored, directed by Josef Von Sternberg, 1931. (The black leather jacket)

Do the Right Thing, directed by Spike Lee, 1989. (Hip hop, Trainers)

Dr. No, directed by Terence Young, 1962. (The bikini)

Foxy Brown, directed by Jack Hill, 1974. (Funk)

Intolerance, directed by D. W. Griffith, 1916. (False eyelashes)

Letty Lynton, directed by Clarence Brown, 1932. (The shoulder pad)

One Million Years B.C. directed by Don Chaffey, 1966. (The bikini)

Quadrophenia, directed by Franc Roddam, 1979. (Mods)

Rebel Without a Cause, directed by Nicholas Ray, 1955. (Jeans, Trainers)

Sabrina, directed by Billy Wilder, 1954. (Celebrities)

Shaft, directed by Gordon Parks, 1971. (Funk)

A Streetcar Named Desire, directed by Elia Kazan, 1951. (The T-shirt)

Superfly, directed by Gordon Parks, 1972. (Funk)

The Wild One, directed by László Benedek, 1953. (The black leather jacket)

Fashion and costume museums

Victoria and Albert Museum (V&A)
Cromwell Road
South Kensington
London SW7 2RL
UK

Fashion Museum
Assembly Rooms
Bennett Street
Bath BA1 2QH
UK

MoMu
Antwerp Fashion ModeMuseum
Nationalestraat 28
B – 2000 Antwerpen
Belgium

Musée des Arts de la Mode
Palais du Louvre
107 rue de Rivoli
75001 Paris
France

Musée de la Mode et du Costume
Palais Galliéra
10 Avenue Pierre 1er de Serbie
75116 Paris
France

Lipperheidesche Kostümbibliothek
Kunstbibliothek
Staatliche Museen zu Berlin
Matthaikirchplatz 6
10785 Berlin
Germany

Costume Institute
Metropolitan Museum of Art
1000 5th Avenue at 82nd Street
New York
NY 10028-0198
USA

Museum at the Fashion Institute of Technology
7th Avenue at 27th Street
New York
NY 10001-5992
USA

Kobe Fashion Museum
9, 2-chome
Koyocho-naka
Higashinada
Kobe 658-0032
Japan

Galeria del Costume
Via della Ninna 5
50122 Florence
Italy

Museum Salvatore Ferragamo
Palazzo Spini Feroni
Via Tornabuoni 2
50123 Florence
Italy

Websites

www.colette.fr

www.firstview.com

www.net-a-porter.com

www.style.com

www.thesartorialist.com

Index

Page numbers in **bold** refer to picture captions

Picture Credits

2 Martin Hayhow/AFP/Getty Images; 8 © The Bridgeman Art Library; 9 Photo by Tony Barson/WireImage/Getty Images; 10 (top) Photo by Arnaldo Magnani/Getty Images; 10 (bottom) Photo by Hulton Archive/Getty Images; 11 © Interfoto/Lebrecht Music & Arts; 12 Photo by Mansell/Tim Life Pictures/Getty Images; 13 Tony Barson/WireImage/Getty Images; 14 Photo by Hulton Archive/Getty Images; 15 Georges Lepape: © ADAGP, Paris and DACS, London 2019; 16 © Emmanuel Fradin/Reuters/Corbis; 17 © 2005 Roger-Viollet/Topfoto; 18 (top) Photo by Lipnitzki/Roger Viollet/Getty Images; 18 (bottom) Photo by Weegee (Arthur Fellig)/International Center of Photography/Getty Images; 19 Courtesy Agent Provocateur; 20 © Bettmann/Corbis; 21 After Sir George Hayter/V&A Images/Victoria & Albert Museum; 22 (top) SNAP/Rex Features; 22 (bottom) Pierre-Philippe Marcou/AFP/Getty Images; 23 (left) © Bettmann/Corbis; 23 (right) Central Press/Getty Images; 24 Condé Nast Ltd – Cecil Beaton/Trunk Archive; 25 (top) Courtesy EMAP; 25 (bottom) © Mary Evans Picture Library 2010; 26 (top) General Photographic Agency/Getty Images; 26 (bottom) Clare Muller/PYMCA; 27 Waring Abbott/Getty Images; 28 The Art Archive/Royal Automobile Club London/NB Design; 29 Alan Band/Keystone/Getty Images; 30 (top) © Bettmann/Corbis; 30 (bottom) dpa Picture-Alliance GmbH; 31 Courtesy PETA; 32 Rob Loud/Getty Images; 33 (top) Slim Aarons/Getty Images; 33 (bottom) © Photo RMN – Ernest Bulloz; 35 Georges Lepape/Vogue © The Condé Nast Publications Ltd; 36 Joel Saget/AFP/Getty Images; 37 Courtesy John Galliano; 38 (left) Photo by Hulton Archive/Getty Images; 38 (right) Paul O'Doye/Getty Images; 39 Library of Congress, Prints & Photographs Division, Russell Patterson, LC-USZCN4-137; 40 © Bettmann/Corbis; 41 The Art Archive/Kharbine-Tapabor/Coll. Galdoc-Grob; 42 © RA/Lebrecht Music & Arts; 43 (left) Bob Thomas/Popperfoto/Getty Images; 43 (right) Syndication International/Getty Images; 44 © Ullstein Bild/Topfoto; 45 Lee Miller/Getty Images; 46 © 2005 Roger-Viollet/Topfoto; 47 Courtesy Shaun Leane; 48 Robert Legon/Rex Features; 49 The Kobal Collection/© catwalking. com; 51(top) Kurt Hutton/Picture Post/Getty Images; 51 (bottom) Startraks Photo/Rex Features; 52 © CHANEL – Collection Denise Tual; 53 (left) The Kobal Collection/United Artists; 53 (right) akg-images; 54 © Man Ray Trust/ADAGP, Paris and DACS, London 2019; 55 catwalking.com; 56 (top) Sipa Press/Rex Features; 56 (bottom) Mark Large/Daily Mail/Rex Features; 57 Eugene Adebari/Rex Features; 58 © V&A Images/Victoria & Albert Museum; 59 catwalking.com; 60 (top) Courtesy Marc Jacobs; 60 (bottom) Courtesy Dior; 61 The Art Archive/Alfredo Dagli Orti; 62 Gjon Mili/Time Life Pictures/Getty Images; 63 (top) catwalking.com; 63 (bottom) The Art Archive/Kharbine-Tapabor; 64 The Kobal Collection; 65 (left) Mike Marsland/WireImage/Getty Images; 65 (right) Everett Collection/Rex Features; 66 Dominique ISSERMANN for the No 5 advertising campaign in 2009 © CHANEL 2009; 67 © Chanel © Andy Warhol Foundation. From Andy Warhol serigraphies.; 68 Margaret Chute/Getty Images; 69 (top) Chris Moorhouse/Getty Images; 69 (bottom) Popperfoto/Getty Images; 70 (top left) catwalking.com; 70 (top right) © Bata Shoe Museum, Toronto 2010; 70 (middle left) catwalking.com; 70 (middle) Getty Images; 70 (middle right) catwalking.com; 70 (bottom left) Courtesy Sergio Rossi; 70 (bottom middle) catwalking.com; 70 (bottom right) © Interfoto/Lebrecht Music & Arts; 71 catwalking.com; 72 Edward Steichen/© Corbis. All Rights Reserved; 73 © RA/Lebrecht Music & Arts; 74 © Steven Meisel/Art + Commerce/Courtesy Yves Saint Laurent; 75 akg-images; 76 (top) © Jerome Albertini/Corbis; 76 (bottom) Ron Galella/WireImage/ Getty Images; 77 © Roger Schall; 78 (top) LAPI/Roger Viollet/Rex Features; 78 (bottom) © John-Paul Pietrus; 79 Rex Features; 80 © RA/Lebrecht Music & Arts; 81 General Photographic Agency/Getty Images; 82 Terry Richardson/Art Partner; 83 (top) Giorgio Armani advertising campaign Autumn/Winter 1984–85 by Aldo Fallai; 83 (bottom) Sasha/Getty Images; 84 akg-images; 85 (top) John Kobal Foundation/Getty Images; 85 (bottom) akg-images; 86 Courtesy Monsoon; 87 (top) Keystone/Getty Images; 87 (bottom) akg-images; 88 Image by Cecil Beaton © Condé Nast Archive/Corbis; 89 (left) © Philadelphia Museum of Art/Corbis; 89 (right) © Salvador Dali, Fundació Gala-Salvador Dalí, DACS, 2019; 90 (top) Photoshot. All right reserved; 90 (bottom) Michael Ochs Archives/Getty Images; 91 © Bata Shoe Museum, Toronto 2010; 92 (left) Eric Ryan/Getty Images; 92 (right) © ADAGP, Paris and DACS, London 2019; 93 catwalking.com; 94 Kurt Hutton/Getty Images; 95 Courtesy Advertising Archives; 96 catwalking.com; 97 (top) Peter Stackpole/Time & Life Pictures/Getty Images; 97 (bottom) © CinemaPhoto/Corbis; 98 © Genevieve Naylor/Corbis; 99 Fred Ramage/Getty Images; 100 Peter Paul Hartnett/Rex Features; 101 (left) Fox Photos/Getty Images; 101 (right) Associated Newspapers/Daily Mail/Rex Features; 102 (left) Gavin Watson/PYMCA; 102 (right) Courtesy Dr Martens; 103 catwalking.com; 104 (top) Lichfield/Getty Images; 104 (bottom) John Chillingworth/Getty Images; 105 © Anthea Simms; 106 (top) Roy Stevens/Time & Life Pictures/Getty Images; 106 (bottom) PA Archive/Press Association Images; 107 Jim Rakete/Photoselection; 108 The Kobal Collection/Danjaq/Eon/UA; 109 Keystone/Getty Images; 110 Rex Features; 111 © Condé Nast Archive/Corbis; 112 © Ullsteinbild/Topfoto; 113 Courtesy Advertising Archives; 114 John Pratt/Keystone Features/Getty Images; 115 © 2006 JapaneseStreets. com/Kjeld Duits; 116 Pascal Le Segretain/Getty Images; 117 (top) Getty Images; 117 (bottom) akg-images; 118 (top) Warner Bros/The Kobal Collection; 118 (bottom) © 2001 Topham Picturepoint; 119 Courtesy Katharine Hamnett & YOOX Group; 120 Courtesy Manolo Blahnik; 121 © Estate Guy Bourdin/Art + Commerce; 122 Courtesy of The Richard Avedon Foundation; 123 (top) © Henry Diltz/Corbis; 123 (bottom) Courtesy Advertising Archives; 124 (top) Keystone/Getty Images; 124 (bottom) Ebet Roberts/Redferns/Getty Images; 125 (main) Courtesy Converse; 125 (top left) Courtesy Nike; 125 (top right) Courtesy Gola; 125 (bottom right) Courtesy Puma; 125 (bottom left) catwalking. com; 126 © Greg Gorman; 127 (top) Carlos Muina/Cover/Getty Images; 127 (bottom) © B.D.V./Corbis; 128 Terry O'Neill/Getty Images; 129 (main) © Ronald Wittek/dpa/Corbis; 129 (inset) © Deborah Feingold/Corbis; 130 Keystone/Getty Images; 131 (top) © Janette Beckman/PYMCA; 131 (bottom) The Kobal Collection/Curbishley-Baird; 132 Reg Lancaster/Getty Images; 133 Clive Arrowsmith/Celebrity Pictures; 134 catwalking.com; 135 (top) © Topfoto; 135 (bottom) Jim Smeal/WireImage/Getty Images; 136 (top) © Condé Nast Archive/Corbis; 136 (bottom) Everett Collection/Rex Features; 137 © Ronald Traeger; 138 akg-images; 139 (main) Rex Features; 139 (inset) Courtesy Advertising Archives; 140 © Peter Knapp; 141 Edward James/Rex Features; 142 (top) Marc Hispard/© Condé Nast Archive/Corbis; 142 (bottom) 2009 Getty Images; 143 Steve Lewis/Getty Images; 144 J. Emilio Flores/Corbis; 145 (top) © Anthea Simms; 145 (bottom) catwalking.com; 146 catwalking.com; 147 Hulton Archive/Getty Images; 148 V&A Images/Victoria & Albert Museum; 149 Courtesy Helen Storey; 150 Keystone/Hulton Archive/Getty Images; 151 (left) George Stroud/Getty Images; 151 (right) © Norman Parkinson/Sygma/Corbis; 152 (top) Contrasto/eyevine; 152 (bottom) Gary Lewis/Polaris Images/eyevine; 153 James Whitlow Delano/Redux/eyevine; 154 McCarthy/Getty Images; 155 (top) Tim Graham/Getty Images; 155 (bottom) © Michael Ochs Archives/Corbis; 156 Everett Collection/Rex Features; 157 Gunnar Larsen/Rex Features; 158 Ilpo Musto/Rex Features; 159 (top) Alan Messer/Rex Features; 159 (bottom) Peter Sanders/Redferns/Getty Images; 160 Berry Berenson © Condé Nast Archive/Corbis; 161 catwalking.com; 162 (top) Courtesy 'Against Malaria' Campaign; 162 (bottom) Francesco Scavullo, Vogue Magazine © Condé Nast Publications; 163 Terry O'Neill/Getty Images; 164 © Bettmann/Corbis; 165 © Bernd G. Schmitz/Corbis; 166 © Derek Ridgers; 167 David Dagley/Rex Features; 168 © Jacob Silberberg/Reuters/Corbis; 169 © Cardinale Stephane/Sygma; 170 (top) © Derek Ridgers; 170 (bottom) © Ted Polhemus/PYMCA; 171 © Lynn Goldsmith/Corbis; 172 © Josh Olins/Trunk Archive; 173 © Inez Van Lamsweerde and Vinoodh Matadin/Trunk Archive; 174 © Janette Beckman/Getty Images; 175 Courtesy Adidas; 176 Lynne Sladky/AP/Press Association Images; 177 (top) © James Lange/PYMCA; 177 (bottom) bigpicturesphoto.com; 178 © Anthea Simms; 179 © Jason Hetherington; 180 Studio Holle-Suppa; 181 Thierry Orban /Sygma/Corbis; 182 (top) Courtesy Stussy; 182 (bottom) Courtesy Staple Design; 183 Jeff Kravitz/Filmmagic/Getty Images; 184 © Billa/Everynight Images; 185 (top) © Derek Ridgers; 185 (bottom) © David Swindells/PYMCA; 186–187 Courtesy Benetton; 188 Ronald Stoops. Maison Martin Margiela A/W 2000–2001, Paris March 2000; 189 © Luc Roux/Corbis; 190 (top) Courtesy Net-a-Porter; 190 (bottom left) Courtesy The Sartorialist; 190 (bottom right) Courtesy John Galliano; 192 © Anne Menke/Trunk Archive; 193 Clive Dixon/Rex Features; 194 Courtesy Muji; 196 © Ian Tilton/Retna; 197 catwalking.com; 198 Chris Jackson/Getty Images; 199 © 2005 AP/Topfoto; 200 Stefano Rellandini/Reuters; 201 Courtesy Adidas; 202 Arnaldo Magnani/Getty Images; 203 Dave M. Benett/Getty Images; 204 Michael Dunlea/Rex Features; 205 Photo by Othello De Souza Hartley/Courtesy Davina Hawthorne; 206 © Kim Kyoung Hoon/Reuters; 207 (top) Toshiyuki Aizawa/Reuters; 207 (bottom) © 2008 J.B. Spector/Museum of Science & Industry, Chicago/Courtesy of Cute Circuit.

Acknowledgements

For Jessie Lindsay

An enormous thank you to Helen Rochester and
Susie May at Laurence King and to Heather Vickers,
Jon Allan and Kirsty Seymour-Ure for all their hard
work and patience. Thank you to Jamie Lindsay and
DW for their expert advice.

First published in 2011
This edition published in 2019
by Laurence King Publishing Ltd
361–373 City Road
London EC1V 1LR

tel +44 20 7841 6900
fax +44 20 7841 6910

e-mail: enquiries@laurenceking.com
www.laurenceking.com

A catalogue record for this book is available from
the British Library.

ISBN: 978 1 78627 390 1

Designed by Two Sheds Design

Picture research by Heather Vickers

Printed in China

Frontispiece: *Alexander McQueen's gold-painted
fox-skeleton wrap, seen at London Fashion Week,
February 2001.*

Harriet Worsley studied fashion at Central Saint Martins
College of Art & Design, where she teaches fashion
communication and fashion journalism. She worked as a
fashion and interiors journalist before starting a career in
garden design. Her previous publications include *Decades of
Fashion*, *The White Dress* and *Classics of Fashion*.